Keeping
the
Team
Going

Keeping the Team Going

A Tool Kit to Renew & Refuel Your Workplace Teams

Deborah Harrington-Mackin

Author of THE TEAM BUILDING TOOL KIT

amacom

American Management Association

New York • Atlanta • Boston • Chicago • Kansas City • San Francisco • Washington, D.C.
Brussels • Mexico City • Tokyo • Toronto

This book is available at a special
discount when ordered in bulk quantities.
For information, contact Special Sales Department,
AMACOM, a division of American Management Association,
1601 Broadway, New York, NY 10019.

This publication is designed to provide accurate and authoritative information in regard to the subject matter covered. It is sold with the understanding that the publisher is not engaged in rendering legal, accounting, or other professional service. If legal advice or other expert assistance is required, the services of a competent professional person should be sought.

Library of Congress Cataloging-in-Publication Data

Harrington-Mackin, Deborah.
    Keeping the team going : a tool kit to renew & refuel your
workplace teams / Deborah Harrington-Mackin.
        p.   cm.
    Includes bibliographical references and index.
    ISBN 0-8144-7008-4 (pbk.)
    1. Work groups.   I. Title.
    HD66.H374   1996
    658.4'036—dc20   95-46817
                                                          CIP

Printing number

10   9   8   7   6   5   4

Contents

96721

• Acceptance vs. Agreement • Gentle Confrontation
• Understanding Personalities • Understanding Group
Behavior • Questions and Answers: Building Strategic
Relationships

Acknowledgments

Six months after the publication of *The Team Building Took Kit*, I found myself talking with my editor over a pay phone in a supermarket where I had stopped briefly as I was driving from one client to another. The editor wanted me to write a book on training. How could I write a book on training, I asked, when everyone I met wanted to know more about working with teams?

I am able to write a second book on teams because of the openness and trust of my clients, who let me work intensely with their various teams. It is from their experience that the material has developed. I extend great appreciation to Dave Archibald and the teams at Specialty Minerals, Terry Ehrich and the teams at Hemmings Motor News, Jim Reilly and the teams at General Cable, and Ray Murray and the teams at RMI. Sometimes I think I live with them more than with my own staff. I also want to thank the teams at JOSTENS in Princeton, Illinois, and Liz Teal and the staff at the Center for the Study of Work Teams at the University of North Texas and the teams at Mother Myricks, the Vermont Department of Corrections, the Town of Bennington, NASTECH, Taconic Plastics, Bijur Lubricating, CHEMFAB, Rutland Regional Medical Center, Wake Robin Continuing Community Care, and Central Vermont Public Service.

I think writing this second book was more difficult than writing the first; maybe raising six children and owning a business is already more than enough to keep me busy. This time I really needed the support and encouragement of some very special people, especially my husband, Paul, who often took on loads of chores to give me book writing time and then graciously read and edited every chapter. Special thanks also go to Lisa Dunbar, who gave me many extra hours of her time to encourage me, do her computer wizardry, and make edits and suggestions, and to my close friends Paula Garret, Dawn Raphan, and Rita Koon, who volunteered to read and comment. I'd also like to pay tribute to my friend and colleague Jean Ann Audy, who before she died often challenged my ideas on the basis of her own experiences with teams. We miss her.

Especially, I want to thank my children—Michael, Sarah, Andrew, Matt, Ben, and Molly—who convince me, more than any group I have ever trained or consulted with, how wonderful it is to be part of their team.

Keeping
the
Team
Going

Introduction

Every fall the University of North Texas Center for the Study of Work Teams has a large conference that attracts teams from all over the world. At a recent conference attendees identified the problems they typically experience once they get beyond the beginning stages with their teams, including:

+ Productivity plateaus
+ Frequent changes in team personnel
+ Changing requirements for skills and competencies
+ Attempts by teams at reverse delegation (giving the work back to someone else)
+ Failure of some members to commit fully to the process in terms of trust
+ Conditional acceptance of teams among employees, especially management
+ A tendency for teams to continue to function as departmental "silos" that are not compatible with a horizontal team structure
+ Difficulty in putting theory into practice while still getting product out the door
+ Sabotage by supervisors and others who have something to lose with the end of the old structure
+ Lack of clarity and understanding about the team leader role
+ Reversion by some members to "old behaviors" after they leave training sessions

These problems, and many ideas about solutions to them, are the topic of this book. Strategies for solving these problems are particularly important to teams because so many forces within and outside organizations are hampering course correction for teams:

- An inflexible organizational infrastructure that does not allow for examination and redefinition
- Unwillingness of both teams and the organization to tackle role and boundary ambiguity
- Narrow and sometimes inaccurate definitions of empowerment
- Changing business conditions
- A tendency to rest on past success
- Old and deeply rooted conflicts among members
- Mixed messages from management because of real or perceived waning of support or commitment
- Emphasis on procedures rather than process and results
- Time limitations

These roadblocks are not insurmountable, but it takes hard work, discipline, and creativity on the part of a team to overcome them.

In *Keeping the Team Going* I relate the experiences of many different types of organizational teams—functional teams such as empowered work groups, self-directed, and cellular teams; cross-functional problem-solving and project teams and multifunctional quality councils; design teams; and interorganizational teams—as they move from their early development to the middle years.*

At some point teams leave the polite and hesitant beginning stage and move on to the ongoing, long-term job of getting the tasks done. Some teams find that they plateau during the second year; others encounter various problems, such as how to rotate leadership, whether everyone should be a leader, whether jobs should be specialized or cross-trained, and what to do when the supervisor doesn't want to train or facilitate.

The "is-that-all-there-is?" stage can have a short lifespan if the team's purpose is to complete a specific task and then disband. For most teams, such as self-directed teams, however, this

---

*The early stages of team development are discussed in my first book, *The Team Building Tool Kit* (New York: AMACOM, 1994).

stage goes on for the life of the team. Often it represents either a blossoming period of increasing accountability and responsibility or a slow erosion of the team's original purpose.

For example, a quality council team in a publishing company had been in existence for nearly three years. During that time, the purpose of the team had shifted from big-picture, customer-focused issues to day-to-day operational decision making without anyone's paying too much attention to the shift. Part of the shift resulted from the CEO's tendency to micromanage; part came from a loss of clarity about focus and a hesitancy to surface the issue. The team members regularly complained outside the meetings about the team, its lack of progress, and the dominance of the CEO in all its actions. The team was clearly floundering.

My task as a consultant was to get the team back on track. Doing this required suggesting modifications to the organizational structure to provide for a big-picture decision-making group and an operational decision-making group. I put together a five-page workbook that focused on identifying the problem, defining the desired state (where they wanted to be), and identifying the structure that would get them there and the particular roles each group would play. I naively anticipated two or three sessions. What transpired was a lengthy process of examining and reexamining the team's willingness to accept responsibility for defining and fixing the problem. In other words, keeping the team going and correcting its course in midstream is not a three-session process!

I've included many stories, both similar to and different from this one, in this book to demonstrate that different teams need different strategies to keep them going. There is no boilerplate that works for every team. Each team must progress through its own development, sometimes with great success and sometimes with much angst and stress.

Keeping the Team Going is designed to share strategies and stories that have worked in real organizations as their teams have moved into the middle stages of development. It can be read as a companion book to *The Team Building Tool Kit*, which was written to get the team up and running, or it can be read on its own.

Keeping the Team Going can be read from cover to cover or used as an easy reference in the middle of a team meeting when a question arises (e.g., "Are there roles for supervisors other than training and facilitating?").

The question-and-answer sections at the ends of the chapters are designed to supplement the chapter material with real-life situations. (Within each chapter, there are highlighted references in the margins to specific questions in the question-and-answer section that pertain to the text at hand. These references provide a quick, handy way to find the question and the answer that refer to the topic being discussed.) We've included questions frequently asked of us as we've helped teams tackle tough issues.

Examples of Team Success

Sometimes it's helpful to know how other teams are doing and the type of results that can be expected. Here is a list of successful teams:

   • Levi sewing plant in Murphy, North Carolina, cross-trained team members to perform thirty-six tasks. Teams run the plant, order supplies, set production goals, and make personnel policy.[1]

   • Edy's Grand Ice Cream teams handle quality and sanitation checks, meet business goals, and control internal scheduling, discipline, training, and career development.[2]

   • S2 Yachts, a Holland, Michigan, boat builder, uses an internal supplier scoring system, a customer-service index that helps internal customers rate the quality of parts and assemblies received from their internal suppliers. The company has reduced large-part finishing time by 65 percent and surface defects by 75 percent and increased small parts yields by 85 percent. Efficiency has improved, allowing the deck team to reduce team size.[3]

   • Allied Signal division in Phoenix boosted factory production by 60 percent and overall labor productivity by 123 percent in fifteen months.[4]

   • Tennessee Eastman Division of Eastman Chemical Company in Kingsport, Tennessee, employs 8,500 people in its manufacturing operations, all of whom serve on at least one team.[5]

• Liebert Corp. an Emergson Electric subsidiary in Columbus, Ohio, improved on-time parts delivery by 20 percent and saved $60,000.[6]

• A team at Texas Instruments in Houston reduced the cost of hazardous waste disposal by $87,000, a savings that represented 70 percent of the total yearly cost of disposing of wastes.[7]

• Started in 1971 as a "greenfield" facility, the Topeka Pet Food factory is America's longest-running team-centered work environment.

• The PHILCO Insurance Company reorganized its technical and clerical employees into structured teams responsible for specific customers. The teams slashed the policy-renewal process from eighty days to twenty-three days and achieved a 79 percent increase in quality, a 79 percent reduction in overtime costs, and a 67 percent decreased in "rush" issuance policies. Productivity increased 140 percent, resulting in a saving of $872,000.

• Eighteen team finalists in the AQP National Team Excellence competition say teams have saved their companies $1.3 million annually by improving effectiveness and cutting waste, reducing accident rates, improving recycling efforts, and creating higher quality products.[8]

• Nearly all U.S. team members (92 percent) receive training and more than half (60 percent) of team members are measured on both individual and team performance. Nearly half (45 percent) of team members surveyed work on a team full time, with overall length of service ranging from one month to nine years.[9]

• Colgate-Palmolive teams in Cambridge, Ohio, are responsible for the entire production process.[10]

• Lake Superior Paper Industries in Duluth, Minnesota, has 350 workers in fifteen teams.[11]

• Self-directed work teams at Sara Lee Knit Products in Gretna, Virginia, posted a 70 percent increase in quality and a 50 percent increase in production.[12]

• GE's Salisbury, North Carolina, plant runs without supervisors and has reduced costs by more than 30 percent, shortened delivery cycles from three weeks to three days, and reduced customer complaints by a factor of ten.[13]

A team is a living organization, with very distinct needs at each stage. The middle stage is a difficult one because it requires consistent hard work; the energizing hoopla that typically occurs at the beginning and the end is missing.

The goal of *Keeping the Team Going* is to provide the encouragement to press on.

Notes

1. Ken Blanchard, "Does Team Management Work?" *Quality Digest* (October 1994): 17.
2. Ibid., p. 17.
3. "Supplier Scoring Keeps Quality Afloat," *Quality Digest* (October 1994).
4. Jack Gordon, "The Team Troubles That Won't Go Away," *Training* (August 1994): 28–29.
5. Ibid., p. 28.
6. Ibid., p. 28.
7. Ibid., p. 29.
8. "Are Teams Worth It?" *Total Quality* 4, no. 5 (May 1993): 8.
9. "Team Tidbits," *Quality Progress* 28, no. 6 (June 1995): 18.
10. Bradlee Thompson, "Negotiation Training: Win or What?" *Training* (June 1991): 33.
11. Ibid., p. 33.
12. Ibid., p. 33.
13. J. R. Katzenbach and D. K. Smith, *The Wisdom of Teams: Creating the High Performance Organization* (Boston: Harvard Business School, 1993), p. 198.

1
Taking On Responsibility

Teams have become the obsession of U.S. organizations in the 1990s. How to start them? Whom to put on them? How to help them grow and flourish? Lakewood Research reports that 73 percent of the organizations polled in its survey have some employees actively involved in teams.[1] However, many of these organizations report mixed results with teams; its taking longer than expected to get the desired results, and not everyone is embracing teamwork as a good thing.

Roles are in a state of flux, causing anxiety among supervisors and managers. Some teams have been launched because it's "the thing to do," not because the creation of a team was the best possible means to an end. Some teams have stumbled and failed; others are thriving. It's an exciting new age of organizational development.

Many new challenges have emerged with the proliferation of teams, including:

- An increasing emphasis among people in the process of creating teams on building relationships rather than on building a strong structure to support the team's development. Without clarity of roles, goals, and procedures, the teams falter.
- Conflicting visions between individual managers who start departmental teams without the agreement of upper management and upper management itself, which may have a very different vision for the company. As the teams lock horns with other departments that are still functioning in a

traditional fashion, no one is quite sure whether to keep the teams going or to disband them.

+ Creation of teams before completion of an analysis of the demand for products or services. Then, when the teams can't produce results quickly enough, they're disbanded. This on-again, off-again strategy ignores the impact that teams have on the organization's culture.

+ Excessively broad, vague, or outdated original statements of purpose and goals for the team. What was created in the beginning doesn't work any more, yet what needs to be done is left unclear. Members are frustrated and confused.

+ A reluctance among some managers to specify what powers they want teams to have, thinking that identifying responsibilities will sound autocratic.

+ Formation of self-directed teams without adequate advance training in on-the-job technical skills. When members experience difficulty, it is perceived as anti-team bias rather than simply frustration over a lack of competency in a particular area.

+ Struggles among management over when to coach and when to direct. Fear and confusion about changing roles interferes with building the strong relationships among managers, supervisors, and teams that are required for successful teams.

+ A belief among professional, nonsupervisory staff (e.g., engineers and computer specialists) that they are part of no team, making it difficult for them to attach to the new culture.

All of these problems are about freedom and control and the development of new relationships between teams and their organizations. What used to be a one-way, top-down relationship has shifted to the give-and-take of a two-way relationship—much more complex, risky, and rewarding.

Taking On More Responsibility

Lawrence Holpp defines empowerment as "the willing and open transfer of resources and power from one level of an organization

to another." Two manufacturing teams in a mining company put it in more down-to-earth terms:
Empowerment is:

+ Taking ownership of your part and your job
+ Making decisions concerning your own department area
+ Adding value to your job
+ Taking responsibility for your decisions
+ Working with other areas to get buy-in
+ Shifting jobs and roles
+ Creating ownership at every level

The teams also found it helpful to define what empowerment is not, especially when some employees took it upon themselves to stop doing an important quality check.
Empowerment isn't:

+ Having the freedom to do whatever you want
+ Giving people the things you don't want to do
+ Disregarding plant policies and existing practices
+ Ignoring commitments to customers
+ Avoiding accontability for results
+ Fixing, rescuing, and giving advice

The empowered workplace, in which teams assume responsibility and ownership for their own success and for the collective success of the organization, recognizes:

+ The customer at the center of all activity
+ The value of all people in and outside the organization
+ The benefit of pooling talent, ideas, and resources to achieve better results
+ The need to take responsibility for one's own actions
+ The importance of rewarding and recognizing the effort of all individuals

In the early stages of team development, responsibility is typically given out in small, measured doses to ensure team success: careful assignment of team roles; brief team meetings; small, achievable goals; and a few supervisory tasks. Occasionally an organization throws caution to the wind and unilaterally converts itself to a team structure overnight, but this is not the norm. Either way, the team's first questions are typically "What are we suppose to do?" and "How are we suppose to do it?" Before we can increase the team's level of responsibility, we have to check that they are clear about their original responsibility.

What Teams Are Responsible for

* Agreeing on an approach to assigned tasks, projects, or problems
* Developing an appropriate process to complete the tasks or projects or resolve the problems
* Performing each step of the process as determined by the team
* Changing the process as needed after measurement and evaluation
* Communicating with all related parties
* Cross-training members to allow for flexible scheduling

Ironically, at this point teams often resist, saying, "We don't get paid enough to carry these jobs. Why is management getting off the hook?" In fact, managers aren't getting off the hook but are finding their own jobs redefined as well.

What Management Is Responsible for

* Sharing the organization's vision, mission, goals, and values
* Coaching and leading the new workforce
* Determining the amount of revenue required and the expense allowed
* Establishing schedules and capacity requirements
* Defining quality standards
* Communicating with all related parties

The management team in a paper-coating company worked for a year as a team with few tangible results. Every week the members met to discuss the quality improvements needed and what was wrong with one system after another. They talked and talked, but nothing changed. The leader became frustrated that few projects had been launched and chastised members for not making the culture change happen. One member spoke up: "I didn't know it was my job to make it happen." The transformation to a team environment requires all roles and all responsibilities to be reexamined, with some being kept from the old style and much that is new being added.

As the organization shifts from its initial launch of teams into expanded responsibility and accountability, resistance to the change will grow. When people can anticipate and prepare for the resistance, they are able to handle it better than when it comes as an unwelcome surprise.

Resistance

Why Teams Resist Responsibility

Teams avoid responsibility for different reasons and in different ways. (See Chapter 2 for more information on resistance.)

Barriers to Responsibility From Within the Team

- Lack of competency/skill to do the task
- Lack of self-confidence
- Fear of failure, ridicule, and criticism
- Fear of being singled out and exposed as incompetent
- Fear of losing approval
- Lack of self-control
- Fear of being put in charge
- Fear of taking responsibility for success or failure
- Fear of change and of the unknown
- Lack of organizational skills
- Fear of being held accountable for mistakes
- Fear of the change success causes in work relationships

Barriers to Responsibility Outside or External to the Team

- Having too many tasks to do in the allotted time
- Experiencing too many changes at the same time

- Having too few people to do the jobs
- Coping with an untrustworthy management
- Coping with management inconsistency (do it, one day; don't, the next)
- Lacking necessary information/resources to do the job
- Having too many bosses to answer to as a result of being a cross-functional team

Barriers like these, within and outside the team, cause some teams to avoid taking on the level of responsibility expected of a maturing team.

How Teams Avoid Responsibility

- Trying to delegate work back to management by suggesting that members don't know how to do the task
- Whining, complaining, fussing, and generally being negative toward anything team-related
- Refusing to do any new task without an attitude
- Doing part of the task and then suggesting that the team ran out of time before completing the task
- "Chasing rabbits" by going off on tangents that drive management crazy

Typical Excuses Teams Use to Avoid Responsibility

- We don't have the right equipment.
- It's too late to start that now.
- If we do it, it probably won't be good enough for them.
- Somebody needs to decide what gets done first around here.

- We're waiting for _____.
- There are just too many things to do right now.
- We've got other problems that need to be tackled first.
- We're totally confused and just don't get it.

The best excuse we've heard for a team's failure to take responsibility for a problem was that the team was initially "too large to accomplish anything." To accommodate the concern about size, the team was divided into smaller subgroups—which were then declared "too small to be of any use at all."

Factors That Help Teams Assume Responsibility

Teams have identified what helps them, both externally and internally, to take on more responsibility.

Components That Influence Teams to Accept Responsibility

+ Existence of adequate support as the team begins work
+ Acceptance of small tasks first with instruction and checkpoints
+ Agreement on common, realistic, and specific goals
+ Tolerance of mistakes and faults
+ Agreement to share concerns with upper management
+ Clarification of priorities and plans from upper management
+ Clear understanding of roles, responsibilities, and decision making
+ Good attitude among team members
+ Adequate resources to do the job
+ Support of other people including family
+ Knowledge and expertise on the team
+ Sense of pride and self-confidence among team members
+ Self-motivated team members
+ Company-wide recognition of successes (small ones as well as major accomplishments)
+ No-nonsense statements about needed behavior change

The amount of resistance teams display varies according to the teams' stage of development. What works for a new team may not be appropriate for a more mature team. Experimentation, open-mindedness, and persistence are essential team behaviors.

The Cycle of Involvement

Researchers have identified a natural "cycle of involvement"[3] that occurs as teams develop. The cycle includes the following six stages: rumors and rumblings, growing awareness, initial action, implementation, integration, and then—perhaps most surprising—diminishing support, particularly when people don't see any personal gain for the extra responsibility involved. There is a tendency among leaders facing resistance to try to push harder and faster toward the goal. As a consequence, the resistance grows. A better strategy is to slow down and go for depth in the stage where the resistance is occurring. Here is a step-by-step plan for handling resistance:

1. Measure the amount of resistance, and decide if you are moving too fast.
2. Slow down, and identify where the team is on the cycle of involvement.
3. Listen to what the resistance is saying. What are the arguments, concerns, gripes, and silence trying to tell you?
4. Instead of pushing ahead, go for depth in the current or previous stages. Provide more information. Be certain information is based on truth, not hype.
5. When in doubt, back up to awareness by providing more information and tools.
6. Understand that anything can interrupt the cycle and be prepared to restart the cycle.

A human resources manager was frustrated when a member of a secretarial team indicated that she didn't feel comfortable offering her suggestion for reorganizing the workload to the team. After much coaxing and coaching, she still refused to talk about her idea. The HR manager, exasperated by the woman's foot dragging, decided to forget the whole idea and just move the team ahead—until he reviewed the cycle of involvement and realized that his strategy was a mistake. Moving ahead would have increased the woman's level of resistance and caused others to join in her resistance, believing that the HR manager was forcing them to move ahead too fast.

Throughout the cycle of involvement, management must anticipate that the team will make mistakes. Without management's tolerance for those mistakes, the team will not continue to accept more responsibility. Nothing kills empowerment faster than fear of reprisal. What are the conditions under which management should tolerate team mistakes?

Guidelines for Accepting Team Mistakes

The following list was generated by a group of managers and supervisors as they wrestled with their own personal issues surrounding mistakes. They decided that it's okay for the team to make a mistake when:

- It doesn't have significant negative impact on the company
- It's a first-time mistake, not part of a pattern
- Team members were working outside of the team's responsibilities
- The team member was following explicit instructions or following the proper procedures
- The team member was working with shared equipment that is not always available
- The team learns from the mistake and is able to say how to avoid it in the future
- The mistake occurred within the scope of the team's authority in pursuit of the goal
- The team was really trying to do it right
- The team's actions were consistent with laws and policies of the company
- Misinformation was given to the team
- The team was taking initiative and risk-taking
- Written procedures weren't clearly defined
- Different skill and ability levels of team members caused erratic results
- There were extenuating circumstances (i.e., extreme or new hardship at home) a death in the family
- The situation was outside the person's control
- The error was not caused by negligence or lack of action
- There were time restraints
- There was poor training

The list was quite extensive and demonstrated to the group that a supportive environment would be more effective to achieve increased responsibility than a punitive one.

Sharing More Responsibility: The Empowerment Hand-Off Plan

The sharing of responsibility requires a systematic plan of delegating work in order to empower team members. This process begins with the empowerment hand-off plan, a step-by-step process for giving increasing responsibility to a team. Before the plan is created, the manager or supervisor must address a series of preliminary questions.

Preliminary Empowerment Questions for the Manager

1. What results are we trying to achieve at this stage in the team's development?
2. What jobs must be done to achieve these results? Who typically performs these tasks? Are there new tasks that will need to be done? Can some tasks be eliminated? (See extended list of tasks in Chapter 2.)
3. Which jobs should management or a specialist do?
4. Which jobs should management give to the team? How much can the team actually perform? What are the team's strengths and weaknesses? How many "sign-offs" do they need?
5. Which team is ready to handle the job?
6. What performance standards must be maintained?
7. How can we build in flexibility? Is cross-training a possibility?
8. What tricky aspects of the job might cause difficulty for the team? What priorities might cause confusion or conflict with departmental or individual members' priorities?
9. How will we monitor the delegated jobs? How will we handle roadblocks the team encounters?
10. Do we need a time cushion?
11. What rewards (praise, thanks, bonuses) will be given?

Q&A
#3

Q&A
#2

Q&A
#13

12. What rules might need to be broken?
13. Are we willing to commit to doing what the team collectively decides?
14. How much authority should the team be given?

Let's suppose that this is a two-year-old team about to be handed the task of developing preliminary budget materials. Although the manager or supervisor might lead the discussion, it is certainly appropriate for the entire team to be involved in exploring and answering these questions.

Steps in the Empowerment Hand-Off Plan

1. Define the task to be delegated to the team. Be sure the task is clear, specific, and attainable.

   Q&A #14

2. Identify the team's level of willingness to take responsibility for handling the task. Responsiveness to answering the preliminary questions should be an indicator of the team's willingness to take on a new task.
3. Define the task clearly to the team, including a description of the tasks to be undertaken and the expected results, important background information, and a discussion of how the task fits into the big picture.
4. Identify the level of skill needed to complete the task and the level of skill the team currently possesses to complete the task; identify the training needed. If training is not an option, consider adding others to the team to get the expertise needed.
5. Check that written procedure exists for the task; consider creation of a subteam to develop procedures if none exist.
6. Identify the amount of authority the team has. For example, should the team:
   a. Investigate the problem and report the details, with management to decide what to do?
   b. List the alternatives available, with the pros and cons of each, with management to decide which to select?
   c. Recommend a specific plan of action for management's approval?
   d. Communicate what the team intends to do and delay action until management approves?

    e. Communicate what the team intends to do and do it unless management says not to?

    f. Take action and let management know what the team did and how it turned out?

    g. Take action and let management know the results only if the result is unsuccessful?

    h. Take action, with no communication necessary?

7. Identify what outside resources are available for the team (time, tools, skills, authority).

8. Discuss pertinent organizational policy that may impact the team's ability to carry out the task. Identify situations to avoid, including where one team's responsibility stops and another team's starts.

9. Identify the scope of responsibility so that the team knows how far it can go within the organization's structure and, if relevant, outside the structure to other organizations.

10. Identify what factors will be used to evaluate the team's performance.

11. Identify the type and frequency of communication required.

12. Discuss the team's plan to carry out the task; ask questions and alert members to possible pitfalls.

13. Explain to other teams why this team was given the responsibility. If appropriate, suggest that other important jobs will be assigned to the other teams in the near future.

One team experienced the problem of an incomplete hand-off plan when it became clear that team members did not know how to perform certain tasks that were handed off to them. Rather than surface their lack of knowledge, the team became hostile toward management and attempted to undercut the team's success. After management recognized that the issue was competency, additional training and temporary hands-on support quickly corrected the problem.

Sometimes resistance is a competency issue; sometimes the team just doesn't want to take on the new responsibility.

Part of the job of getting the team to take on more responsibility is to create a shift in focus from members' fears to their desires. Researchers have found that this subtle shift in thinking from the negative to the positive can dramatically impact outcomes. To accomplish such a shift:

- Encourage the team to identify specific fears, problems, and risks associated with taking on a new task.
- Sort the fears into those that the team can control and those it can't.
- Do not judge the fears (e.g., "You shouldn't feel that way.").
- For items that the team cannot control, identify a team or person with control so that the team can share these concerns with someone who can help.
- For items that the team does control, identify a strategy that the team could use to assume control (e.g., begin cross-training, tell someone about the problem).
- For each strategy identified, have members write their desired outcome on pieces of paper.
- Share the strategies and outcomes among all members.

Confronting Refusal to Take Responsibility

Sometimes getting more out of a team requires confronting members about their refusal to take on more responsibility. It's necessary to challenge the team's assumptions and fears in a direct and open manner. As the team members respond, the manager must do the following:

- Listen to their point of view.
- Ask many questions to uncover the root of their refusal.
- Sort the truths from the untruths.
- Define what management will and won't do.
- Offer training resources and encouragement.
- Avoid expressing resentment and threatening punishment for failure.
- Continue to share information freely rather than withholding.
- Use any new team effort to build members' confidence.

We have found with some manufacturing teams that the manager periodically has to give the "yes, we will do this" talk. It's the result of an automatic testing response among members. They want to be certain that commitment isn't waning before they venture out on a limb and try something new or different.

Reversing Reverse Delegation

Occasionally when the work is delegated or the team makes an error, members will try to delegate the task back to the original person. It's called "passing the monkey." To prevent this:

1. Make sure the team is properly equipped with the skills to do the job.
2. Talk about the value of and the need for risk taking; say that you recognize problems may occur. The adage "You can't get to second base with your foot still on first" might help to encourage risk taking.

3. Do proper resource planning in terms of time, tools, skills, and authority.
4. Clearly communicate expectations to the team, explaining how its performance will be evaluated and what you will and won't do to assist the team to overcome weaknesses.
5. Focus on the work that is being done correctly, and limit reinforcement of work done incorrectly.
6. When approached by the team with an expectation that you will drop everything and respond right now, reply that you are interested in the problem and will discuss it at a time convenient for both of you, unless it is essential to discuss it right now.
7. Encourage the team to think about the problem and prepare possible solutions for any future discussion.
8. Make statements that clearly indicate that you think the team can and should make decisions.
9. Make it clear that you expect the team to make the final decision within a specified time frame.

Difficulty With Delegating

Most managers have set ways for how they think tasks should be performed. When a team approaches the task differently or doesn't do it fast enough, management may find it tempting to take back the responsibility that has already been delegated to the team. This tug of war can go on for months, in effect keeping the team stuck in its development.

Among the reasons some managers choose not to delegate to the team are these:

- Worry about being held accountable for something that the manager can no longer control
- Perceived importance of the decision
- Reluctance to share power
- Disbelief that the team will actually deliver
- Worry that the team will "show the manager up"
- Too much personal investment in success
- Need to feel indispensable
- Concern that the team will find past mistakes
- Reluctance to admit that other people may know more than the manager does
- Concern about who will get the credit
- A need to be liked that is greater than the need to have team carry its proper share of the workload

When a team is waiting to get assignments and the manager is reluctant to give responsibility or is not skilled at delegating responsibility, here are some specific items for the team to double-check:

- Find out the team's level of authority, using the earlier list on page 17. If the team's manager is reluctant to give authority, write up the team's plan and submit it to the manager with a bold "Unless we hear from you . . ." statement.
- Repeat the instructions given to the team to be certain they were understood correctly.
- Ask for specific deadlines for each part of the project or task.
- If multiple tasks are given at the same time, ask the manager to prioritize the tasks for the team.
- Question how well the task should be done. Perfectly? Just a draft?

It doesn't take a team long to realize that the shifting of responsibility is a benefit to management, giving managers and supervisors more time for planning and technical projects as they are relieved of more mundane tasks. For team members who carry all their new team duties, the hoopla of team building quickly fades. Yet organizations have been slow to develop the necessary reward systems to support shared responsibility.

Keeping the Environment Ripe for Responsibility

Part of the willingness of members to assume more responsibility is based on the reality of what they will get back in return. If being a team member simply means more hard work, the level of support will wane. Members must experience benefits, both tangible and intangible, if responsibility is to take hold. They lose interest and a sense of responsibility when they don't see how their extra effort will pay off.

New Ideas About Rewards and Recognition

More and more research is being done on team rewards and recognition. There is a clear realization that both the individual and the team need to share in the reward process. Typical measures of team performance involve four different areas:

1. Individual team members' ability to do more tasks
2. The personal performance level of the individual team members
3. The team's overall performance level
4. The team's performance as compared to that of other, similar teams

What's in It for Me?

As team members are asked to take on more responsibility, their first question is "What's in it for me?" Compensation plans and reward and recognition programs have lagged far behind the growth of the team movement. As more organizations experiment with team-pay systems, however, certain information has become known. Base pay and indirect pay have little reward value for teams because they do not use meaningful quality measures or encourage high-performance work teams, whereas variable pay or incentive pay is flexible and provides powerful rewards for organizational teams.

The value of team incentives is that they:

- Reward and reinforce team excellence
- Explain what benefit teamwork has for people
- Help control payroll costs while providing motivational payouts for bottom-line results
- Use a wide variety of qualitative and quantitative measures
- Adapt to changing direction as specific circumstances change

Guiding Principles for an Incentive Plan Design

There are a number of basic principles to keep in mind when establishing a compensation systems for teams. They include these points:

- Pay for results on the basis of goal achievement.
- Tie incentives to real bottom-line gains for the business unit in order to make the plan self-funding.[4]
- Add to the competitive base salary without decreasing merit pay.
- Pay incentives and bonuses promptly, preferably weekly.
- Keep the plan simple so that employees can see how they affect the achievement of goals.
- Correlate goal difficulty to payouts so that payouts fit the level of accomplishment.
- Involve employees in plan design, goal setting, implementation, and evaluation of success.
- Measure actual results for operational measures against the baseline goal.
- Reduce or eliminate payouts if overall financial performance is low, regardless of cause, to protect business viability and job security better.

- Set incentive ranges at from 3 to 10 percent, with ten percent typically being the cap.
- Limit the number of measures for the incentive plan to approximately five (e.g., quality of work, schedule, profitability, productivity, customer satisfaction).
- Communicate about financial measurement and progress toward goals.
- Pay for individual results by providing a base pay that is the same for all members of teams where members all have equivalent roles but little interaction and then adding results-based merit pay on top.
- Use conventional job-based pay or skill-based pay for supervised teams where work occurs in a prescribed order.
- Use the same team merit pay for self-managed teams where performance depends upon coordination among all members.[5]
- Treat underachievers as a management issue, not a compensation issue.
- Benchmark with pacesetters to gain a strong external focus on how exceptional organizations perform.
- Reflect a combination of external competitiveness and skill-or-knowledge-based pay in any base pay. The team assessment often totals 20 percent of the pay.
- Avoid traditional merit plans that reward individual performance.
- Make executives economic partners with team members by including a combination of long- and short-term team measures in executive pay programs.[6]
- Use a transition pay program (temporary umbrella, draws, or guarantees) for sales teams to lessen the impact of the new program for some people; typically they cost 1 to 5 percent of total cash compensation for a sales force.
- Look for "cost-neutral" plans (where compensation budgets do not exceed those for the previous year) that still drive higher levels of performance.
- Use level of discretion and judgment as primary job factors, with impact, number contacts, supervision, and all other factors as secondary.[7]

Sample Team-Based Incentives

The important question to ask here is "What results is the team trying to achieve?" Be certain to emphasize measures that support teams; pay is a reinforcer or consequence that either strengthens or weakens team behavior. Team environments need to stress customer satisfaction, responsibility for quality, team accomplishments, effective communication, and problem solving and decision making. Some examples of team-based incentives are:

- A sales-growth bonus that is distributed to all team members on the basis of the number of hours worked
- A payment equaling 25 percent of the cost reductions achieved
- A 7 percent incentive given for completion of specific training requirements
- A 3 percent grant award based on team performance
- A 25 percent of bonus payout based on a 2 percent increase in overall customer satisfaction from the previous year's results
- An exchange of 10 percent of salary for a bonus pegged to achieving company goals, including improved customer satisfaction, employee satisfaction, revenue, and profit
- A payment of any percentage that focuses on improvement and performance, not entitlement (e.g., by tying pay to customer satisfaction survey results)
- The withholding of 5 percent of base pay until the entire organization has completed mandatory annual training

Q&A #10

Team Participation as Extra Credit

In some companies, employees may participate on problem-solving or project teams once or twice a year. This contribution can be included as "extra credit" on the traditional performance appraisal.

Team Awards

Q&A #9

Many team-based organizations are still struggling to decide what to do about their old award programs, such as awards for years of service, in the new team environment. Some are finding it best to keep the old system intact and supplement it with new elements of team awards. Team awards should:

- Acknowledge behavior that the team has designated as worthy of reward
- Involve the team in determining the types of rewards that are most meaningful to them
- Be consistent within teams and among teams
- Be given in a timely, public manner

- Build self-esteem of all team members
- Support what the organization values (e.g., customer service, good achievement, risk taking, cutting costs)
- Be based on clearly defined criteria
- Give everyone an equal opportunity to be recognized

Examples of team awards and celebrations are:

- Posters, letters, or other forms of recognition
- New equipment, furnishings
- Public recognition at company-wide meetings
- Presentations to management
- Special t-shirts, mugs, or other memorabilia
- Team attendance at a function or event
- Displays of works in progress—charts, etc.
- Photo displays of team members at work
- Short videos of the team in action to show to others in the organization
- An article about the team in a company newsletter
- A visit or call from the organization's top leadership

One of the beauties of teams is their ability to generate many terrific ideas for acknowledging their accomplishments. We've seen skits, videos, lifesize posters, even two employees who dress up as old ladies—Myrt and Ethel—and wander around the company visiting with employees and cheering on their efforts with teams. Truly, the ideas are endless.

QUESTIONS AND ANSWERS:
Taking On Responsibility

1. **Q.** *Are there certain characteristics that make some people accept responsibility more than others?*

   A. Yes. Researchers have found that the following characteristics are more prevalent in empowered people: a desire to be empowered, personal and interpersonal awareness and openness, commitment, willingness to take risks, high self-esteem, strong ethical base, patience, self-motivation, and an assumption of responsibility.[8] Most of these characteristics can be developed in people over time.

2. **Q.** *We changed to self-directed teams overnight, and responsibility was heaped on us. How are we suppose to manage it?*

   A. I've heard a number of stories in which managers have come in and announced without warning that the organization is shifting to self-directed work teams. One even instructed her staff to figure out who would be on each team, what their jobs would be, how often they would meet, and so on. The result was an unnecessary nightmare. Team members picked their friends, and instantly twenty-three cliques were formed. To answer your question, I would go back and create a team charter and a hand-off plan that identifies exactly what the team is accountable for, specific work tasks, and the level of skill required to complete the tasks. Then identify the skill level of the team (what it does and doesn't know), and share the information with management. Also, don't forget the importance of defining new goals, team roles, and team procedures.

3. **Q.** *What do we do when there is so much emphasis on multiskilling on our team that we lose mastery over anything?*

   A. Obviously, it's important to provide training and certification processes to achieve mastery levels. However, when people are expected to do five or six jobs, mastery gets lost. Many teams debate whether everyone on the team needs to be skilled in all tasks. I've seen success both ways, so do what works for your team.

4. **Q.** *Sometimes a team member will come to me as a supervisor and ask for advice on how to handle a situation. After I give a suggestion or two, the person keeps shooting all my ideas down saying, "That won't work because . . ." How do I get this person to fix his own problem?*

A. A manager and I had this same problem with a team member who couldn't get along with another team member. He came looking for advice, and we gave him our best opinion. He immediately said, "No, no, you see . . ." The manager responded with a second suggestion, then a third, and so on. Finally, I said, "Look, we've given you four suggestions, and you've ruled out each one. I'm not certain you want to fix this problem. Why don't you go think about it, then identify the suggestion you like best and come back, and we'll help you work on it." He tried to engage again, but we held firm.

5. **Q.** *Aren't teams willing to take more risks than individuals?*

A. Research does suggest that groups of people are more willing to take risks than individuals (see Chapter 4). It's one of the reasons that teams must be careful to avoid groupthink (when all the team members quickly agree with each other and don't oppose or challenge other viewpoints).

6. **Q.** *Why don't people want to take on more responsibility? Doesn't it make the job more exciting?*

A. Empowerment involves loss as well as gain. People give up the following: things they feel comfortable with, the ability to blame, individuality, security, control, routine, the safety zone, old rules, old stature. On the other hand, they do experience gains: control over their own destiny, a better sense of the business, increased knowledge and respect, more involvement and awareness, increased self-worth, and more flexibility. Sometimes people see the losses more clearly than the gains because the loss column is more tangible and concrete. The team has to show how the gains will more than balance the losses if it wants members to share responsibility.

7. **Q.** *What do you do when the whole team tries to resist taking on more responsibility?*

   A. There is a good video called *Group Tyranny and Gunsmoke Phenomenon* (CRM Films). I like to show it because it talks about how decisions can be influenced by the group, even to the point where people go against their own values just to belong to the group. At this point, the agreement manager (the sheriff) emerges to tell the group to back off. When a group is really tyrannical, it needs an agreement manager who will draw a line in the sand that can't be crossed.

   However, drawing a line in the sand when there is no tyranny will backfire. A company president during his annual presentation to a team-structured division said, "Our motto for the future is 'Lead, follow, or leave.' " Rather than being a rallying cry, the motto elicited a resounding thud.

8. **Q.** *Isn't it okay to reward individuals in teams?*

   A. There is no problem recognizing the accomplishments of individual members of a team as long as their reward is not the result of a collective effort. Given that most accomplishments require the help of other people, it is best to reward the team as a whole—and reward all the individual people on the team as well.

9. **Q.** *In our organization, we choose the best quality team, the best customer satisfaction team, and so on. Is that okay?*

   A. Experts caution about setting up a recognition system that creates internal competition between teams. When teams are competing against each other, they have their eye off the real competition. Besides, internal competition is contrary to the concept of internal customer and strategic partnerships. Better to work as a whole organization against your real competitor.

10. **Q.** *Most of the traditional job factors for compensation reward years of service, level of authority, and independent action. These don't seem to be appropriate in a team environment. What types of factors would you use for the compensation of people who work on teams as part of their job?*

A. When it comes to job factors, I usually suggest incorporating a TQM focus that includes teams but adds in customer service, quality, and other factors that are not traditionally measured. Examples of such factors are:

* *Customer focus.* Customer focus measures the amount of contact with the external customer, ranging from the occasional contact to front-line customer service and/or sales. Examine the level of accountability for satisfying customer needs, the value-added nature of the position in relationship to the customer for each position, and responsibility for maintaining the relationship.

* *Team participation.* Team membership measures the extent to which the job requires participation on company-wide and departmental teams where collaborative and collective effort are required. Team participation can range from departmental operation or project teams to company-wide planning or policy teams.

* *Quality.* Quality measures the level of responsibility for delivering the required quality level, the amount of impact directly on the customer, and the level of responsibility for measuring and/or ensuring measurement of quality, zero defects, failure costs, and so on.

* *Process knowledge.* Extent of job knowledge, technical and/or professional skill, and ability to meet changing situations; knowledge of multiple jobs, adherence to standard work processes and procedures; use of TQM data devices.

* *Technical systems.* Level of required skill in the development and/or use of technology; required amount of learning of new skills; forecasting and anticipating skills.

* *Problem-solving and analytical skills.* Degree to which the job requires anticipation of potential problems; ability to de-

velop alternatives and explore full range of choices and to recommend ideas, alternatives, and solutions.

+ *Leadership.* Extent to which the position causes others to perform in ways that produce desired results.

For more information on team compensation, I recommend Steven Gross's book, *Compensation for Teams.*[9]

11. **Q.** *What do you do when certain people are unwilling to fulfill their responsibility as a member of a team?*

 A. In the traditional culture the supervisor had a tendency to cover up performance problems. In a team environment, however, there is no longer anyone protecting the poor performer. After a period of time, most teams become very intolerant of people who don't carry an equal share of the workload. A well-functioning team will have a member speak individually with the person about taking more responsibility. If the member doesn't respond after one or two requests, the problem should be discussed by the whole team.

12. **Q.** *Should team members assess one another's performance as a way of determining compensation?*

 A. It takes a very mature team to talk about compensation and individual performance. One team succeeded very well discussing how to divvy up a quarterly bonus based on performance. They established key performance measures (hours worked, quantity produced, quality rating) and used them to determine the bonus allocation. However, a new team probably would be unable or unwilling to make compensation decisions.

13. **Q.** *As a manager who would like to empower his staff, what can I do in a traditional environment that won't end up creating cultural chaos?*

 A. I'm glad to see that you recognize that shifting to a higher level of empowerment is a culture shift. When a single department tries to be different from everything around it, it becomes very difficult for the people who have become more empowered. They have difficulty interacting with traditional managers and supervisors who try to keep them "in their place." My best advice is to begin to talk about the results that other organizations are achieving with teams and then try to get other managers to jump on the bandwagon.

14. **Q.** *When creating a hand-off plan, should I start with an easier task to build the team's confidence or a more important and difficult task to gain their commitment?*

   A. I'd start with the tasks they already are involved in and increase their level of empowerment bit by bit. If you take a task that is brand new to them and is also very important to the organization, the stakes become too high, which causes the resistance to increase. People need to believe they can be successful in order to take on something new.

Notes

1. *Total Quality Newsletter* 5, no. 1 (January 1994): 2.
2. Lawrence Holpp, "Applied Empowerment," *Training* (February 1994): 39.
3. Rick Maurer, "A Pillar of Strength," *TQM Magazine* (September/October 1993).
4. D. O'Neill and D. Lough, "Team Incentives and TQM," *ACA Journal* (1994).
5. Edilberto Montemayor, "A Model for Aligning Teamwork and Pay," *ACA Journal* (1994).
6. J. Schuster and P. Zingheim, "Building Pay Environments to Facilitate High Performance Teams," *ACA Journal* (Spring/Summer 1993): 40–51.
7. Donald V. Brookes, "Designing Quality Compensation Systems," *Quality Digest* (April 1995): 49–50.
8. J. Vogt and K. Murrell, *Empowerment in Organizations: How to Spark Exceptional Performance* (Pensacola, Fla.: Pfeiffer, 1990).
9. Steven E. Gross, *Compensation for Teams* (New York: AMACOM, 1995).

2
Getting Back on Track

Getting back on track requires shifting from being powerless to being empowered, from waiting for orders to taking action, from being reactive to being proactive, from placing blame on others to problem solving. It means revisiting the vision, mission, values, and goals—lighting a fire under the team again. Teams that are able to accomplish their goals and maintain relationships have distinctive characteristics that other teams lack.

Key Characteristics of High-Performance Teams

- Obsession with the external customer
- Emphasis on continuous improvement
- Focus on both process and end results
- Acknowledgment of the changing roles for people within the organization (see Chapter 8 for new role definitions)
- Emphasis on increased responsibility of supervisors to help in new ways in the organization
- Acknowledgment of the need for change
- Skill at gathering and analyzing data critical to the team
- Willingness to change from an obedience-and-order model to one of empowerment
- A common vision and well-defined goals
- Strong respect and trust between members

Realigning a Team

A large Quality Council found itself going through the motions for over a year. It decided to divide up into six subteams that worked for six months reexamining the organization's vision, values, mission, goals, structure, and roles. The process took them deep into the heart of the organization and included the following number of steps to get back on track. Other teams faced with a new task or the need to fix an existing problem may find this approach helpful:

1. Come to an agreement on a clear statement of the problems the team is experiencing.

2. Identify as a team the team's goal or the desired outcome of the reexamination.

3. Gather data and feedback from others in the organization about the problem and the goal. The focus questions: Are we on target with the problem? Is it worth our while to work on the problem and this goal?

4. Subdivide the team, particularly if the team is large, into small working subteams. Each sub-team develops specific items to be accomplished (e.g., draft of values statement by certain date; clarification of management's role). Each subteam has at least one leader selected by the team and rotates facilitation needs.

5. Hold regular meetings of all subteam leaders to maintain connections between the subteams and to address common questions and concerns (e.g., should our subteam work beyond a one-year focus?). About halfway through, the subteams may restructure to make different combinations.

6. Have each subteam select a member to be part of a "synthesis team" that works on draft statements or any tasks that affect all the subteams and relate to the goal.

7. Once a month have the whole team meet to "test the recipes." Realistic hypothetical situations can be identified, and the team can use the results of the subteam work to determine if the draft materials are working to fix the problems identified earlier. The whole team should communicate the results of its work to the rest of the company. Communication may be done via company-wide meetings, a company newsletter, a traveling "road show" to departmental meetings, or other methods.

8. Select a project coordinator early in the process to help facilitate subteam discussions, check for duplication of effort, benchmark with external companies, and coordinate meetings.

The teams at a large propane gas distributorship reached their plateau after a two-year period and wanted to explore ways to improve their effectiveness. The organization used excellent measurement systems with the teams to identify specific goals. For example, the warehouse team members were each assigned a specific target area (e.g., receiving, housekeeping, accuracy) to track results, which were reported to the team each week.

Conducting a Team Assessment

If, despite the measuring, a team is having difficulty, it may be helpful to conduct an assessment of the following sixteen areas:

1. *Organizational alignment.* Does the team have written statements of vision, values, mission (purpose), structure, roles, and goals? Was a team charter ever made for the team? Has the charter been revisited to determine if the ground rules have changed?

2. *Goal clarity.* Are there clearly stated common goals? Are the goals current? Do action plans exist to meet the goals?

3. *Leadership.* Is leadership shared? How much is management still controlling the actions of the team?

4. *Roles.* Have roles been defined on the team? Are the roles such as facilitator, process observer, scribe, timekeeper, and team leader regularly rotated? Are too few people doing too many roles?

5. *Norms.* Have the teams defined their rules (help/hinder list)? Do the teams regularly review compliance with their rules?

6. *Team participation.* Who are high participators? Who are low participators? What causes shifts to appear? Are tasks equally shared?

7. *Team meetings.* Is an agenda constructed by members and distributed before each meeting? Does the team prioritize the agenda and commit to time frames before beginning the meeting? Are meeting dates and times regular and in an appropriate loca-

tion? Does the meeting start and end on time? Are previous action plans reviewed and revised? Are facilitators skilled at helping the team reach decisions? Is progress achieved in the meetings? Do members clarify what they need from each other?

8. *Competency to perform tasks.* Are members cross-trained on work and team tasks? Have competencies been identified?

9. *Communication.* Is communication open, honest, and direct? Do members give each other constructive feedback? Do nonverbal behaviors (gestures, eye direction, posture) indicate any problems?

10. *Atmosphere.* What is the team atmosphere (warm, hostile, dependent, confronting, accepting, low-energy)? What behaviors characterize the description? What is needed to change the atmosphere? What is needed to change the nonproductive or negative behaviors?

11. *Decision-making.* Does the team check its authority level before entering the decision process? Does the team achieve consensus, making decisions that all members can live with and behaviorally support? Does the team look for mutually supported alternatives when striving to achieve consensus?

12. *Problem solving.* Is the team able to delay judgment and encourage the expression of new ideas? Does the team leap from problem to solution too quickly? Is the team using total quality management, reengineering, or other sound problem-solving tools (brainstorming, flowcharting, pareto and cause and effect diagrams, decision trees and matrices)? Does the team assume authority for forming, modifying, and carrying out its processes?

13. *Conflicts.* Who are the team members who tends to agree and support one another on the team? Who are the people who seem the most "in," and why? Who seem the most "out"? Are those who are "out" influencing the team in a negative way? How are feelings handled by the team (expressed, suppressed, ignored)? Has the team determined a protocol for how it will handle conflicts?

14. *Performance management.* Do members still ask "What's in it for me?" What reward systems have been identified, and how often are they used? Do the reward systems benefit individuals or the team as a whole, or both? How is performance measured?

What control systems are in place? Does the team manage its own performance, or is management still managing performance?

15. *Work tools and training.* Has training continued beyond the initial team training? Does the team periodically assess what refreshers are needed? Does the team have an active support mechanism (e.g., team champion, resource team) or resources available to help address questions and problems?

Q&A #3

16. *Boundary management.* Does the team do a good job of developing relationships with other teams, customers, suppliers, and key stakeholders in other parts of the organization?

Each of these areas identifies spots where the team can become disconnected from its process. In the case of the propane gas distributorship, the disconnections occurred around the areas of managing conflicts, problem solving, and decision making. The teams attempted to use their strengths (measuring task achievement) to compensate for their weaknesses. The result was a plateauing of productivity and commitment.

Talking to the Teams About Problems

When the disconnections or ruptures occur, responding with timely help is critical. These steps can be useful:

- Allow teams to vent their frustrations, and identify the most significant obstacles, ruptures, and disconnections.

Q&A #9

- Help team members understand that there will be no punishment for surfacing and discussing problems in depth.
- Work hard at taking blame off individual team members.
- Bring in temporary support personnel to enhance skills, provide necessary competencies, and provide short-term assistance or support.
- Move from identifying the problem to describing the "desired state" in detail. Set realistic, short-term goals.
- Break the desired state into component parts if helpful, and seek active descriptions of each part.
- Look for alignment of vision, values, purpose, structure, roles, and goals.

Q&A #6

- Make managers accountable for coaching and working with the team to help meet members' needs.
- Identify training and retraining needs.
- Create an action plan as a team to get back on track. Include who is responsible for what and target deadlines.
- Plot and monitor key progress milestones. Reward achievement.

A cross-functional planning team found it difficult to write a problem statement that all members could agree on. What worked for them instead was the creation of a circle; members placed their problems either on the rim of the circle (broad-problem categories) or inside the circle (subsets of the broad categories). The visual representation helped members stay focused on the key issues. It also provided the team with a clear diagram of the problems that could be shared with other members of the company. As the solicited feedback from others, team members were able to modify the visual aid very quickly because they did not need to rework any written text.

A similar approach can be used with the radar chart (see Chapter 6); members can plot their impressions of the team's progress on the chart and then develop a composite.

Teams may also get off track because of lack of clarity and understanding of the team leader role. Although no statistical data exist to substantiate the importance of the team leader role to the team's progress, most teams agree that an effective team leader makes a huge difference. Recognizing this fact, many organizations put a strong team member in the role for a long period of time and in effect create a mini-supervisor. When that happens, the team is off track.

The Role of Team Leader

The team leader role, more than any other, is a frequent source of problems for many teams. The struggle usually surrounds the following:

- Who should be a team leader?
- How often should the job be rotated?

- What should the job include?
- How can teams prevent the person from becoming a mini-supervisor?
- If the job is rotated, how do teams adjust to the varying skill levels of the different leaders?
- Does every team leader on every team have to act and do the same things?

Who Should Be Team Leader?

Most teams agree that the job of team leader should be rotated among all members of the team. However, there is a growing body of opinion that argues that some people on teams should not have to be team leaders if they don't want to. We disagree. It is not helpful for strong members of a team to become stronger, leaving weaker members behind. U.S. companies often push for quick results rather than taking the time to improve the skills of weaker members. One process that can be very successful is to put the team leader job on an alphabetical rotation, allowing weaker members to "pass" initially if they wish to and then buddying them up with a stronger member on the third rotation. The buddy assists the team leader as he or she builds skill.

The team leader should be an active member of the team and not necessarily a manager or supervisor. While many organizations include former supervisors or lead people in the team leader rotation, this affects the ability of the other team members to take responsibility for results; dependency on a formal authority is difficult to break.

Team Leader Rotation

Some teams rotate the team leader job as often as weekly or monthly, while others keep the same person in the job for an extended period (six months to a year) in order for the member to really understand the position. The critical issue is to prevent the development of a minisupervisor. That's why we suggest frequent rotation (every one or two weeks). Anticipate that team members will argue about this point, and decide beforehand how important it is to the team's success. It may be that some flexibility is called for.

Adjustment for Skill Level

It should be expected that different members of a team will have different skill levels. Often some members have been temporary supervisors in the former culture, stepping in when the regular supervisor went on vacation. When the team leader role is first given to the team, it is important to identify the competencies required to do the job and to begin to train members on those competencies. Research shows that when team leaders are ill prepared, a certain disorder results among the team.[1] Likewise, when team leaders are respected by members, they are more effective as team leaders. Within three to four rotations of the team leader job, most people have achieved an acceptable level of competency.

Subdividing the Team Leader Job

Some teams report excellent success with subdividing the team leader function into component parts (e.g., production, processes, quality, administration, safety, equipment, customer relations, team relations, supplies and materials, work environment, and training) and then assigning each part to a different person on the team. For example, a team of twelve people could have each member responsible for one of the components and have the team leader function as the coordinator of all the parts. Again, the key is to keep the rotation going so that the strength of one member doesn't become a weakness in the long run because the team comes to depend on it too much.

JOSTENS' Princeton, Illinois, jewelry plant developed a matrix operational structure that identifies the various tasks of the team member overseeing a particular area. Here are some examples:

Administrative Focus Team Member

♦ Code and approve timecards.
♦ Coordinate time and place for team meetings.

- Coordinate vacation schedules.
- Organize and conduct regular team meetings.
- Coordinate selection of new team members.
- Familiarize team with company policies.
- Organize development of team budget.

Quality Focus Team Members

- Complete customer returns data base form.
- Monitor repair orders.
- Determine urgency of quality issues.
- Arrange and conduct team meetings to address quality issues.
- Coordinate incorporation of consistent quality into the process.
- Analyze correlation between internal and external customer expectations, and coordinate development of recommended changes in internal quality standards.
- Analyze returns, reworks, and rejects, and establish team priorities and corrective and preventive action.

Production Focus Team Member

- Initiate, schedule, and conduct production meetings.
- Monitor production costs.
- Monitor and report on production goals.
- Assist team in scheduling decisions.
- Coordinate team's decision on overtime needs.
- Monitor and refine team workflow.
- Attend company-wide production meetings as representative of the team.

Processes Focus Team Member

- Coordinate spec changes, and complete spec change requests.
- Determine urgency of process issues, and arrange for and conduct team meetings to resolve same.
- Solicit prompt team review and approval of manufacturing specs.
- Develop team's troubleshooting capabilities and activities.

+ Organize and conduct process trials.
+ Coordinate team member involvement in capability analysis.
+ Plan and organize team involvement in developing process documentation.
+ Solicit team involvement in initiating and justifying replacement equipment.
+ Coordinate development of new processes and/or processes needed to manufacture new products.

Training Focus Team Member

+ Coordinate the plan, proposal, and schedule of all training.
+ Coordinate identification of training needs.
+ Coordinate training recordkeeping.
+ Monitor and report on training costs.
+ Coordinate new employee orientation.
+ Arrange for team members to conduct training.
+ Coordinate recommendation of outside training support.

Supplies/Materials Focus Team Member

+ Coordinate the pickup of supplies.
+ Coordinate the logging of supply usage.
+ Coordinate the initiation of requisitions for supplies.
+ Coordinate supply inventory.
+ Assist in monitoring material and supply costs.
+ Coordinate with vendors to reduce supply and material variation and problems.
+ Coordinate income inspection—vendor certification.

Work Environment Focus Team Member

+ Initiate accident reporting.
+ Monitor safety practices.
+ Shut down equipment (end of shift).
+ Coordinate housekeeping activities.
+ Implement and maintain Total Productive Maintenance.
+ Assist in eliminating hazardous materials.
+ Recommend ergonomic improvements.
+ Monitor costs.

Customer Relations/Tours Focus Team Member

- Coordinate general communication within and outside the team.
- Coordinate and/or conduct visitor tours of the team.
- Coordinate team preparation and/or participation in customer/sales rep visits.
- Determine urgency of customer relations issues; arrange for and conduct team meeting to resolve them.
- Coordinate customer/supplies relations.
- Coordinate establishment of help/hinder list.
- Coordinate the handling of relationship issues and questions.
- Check to be certain process observer role is used on team.

Within each of the component parts, JOSTENS identified the key competencies to be achieved and targeted a three-phase process for bringing all teams up to speed.

JOSTENS extends the component parts one step by assigning a former supervisor (who is now called a team development leader) to each of the components (see Chapter 8). Each former supervisor is responsible for one of the components for all twenty or so self-directed teams. The team development leader overseeing administration can gather all the team members who oversee administration on the individual teams to provide quick information or problem solving. Managers are on the horizontal of the matrix with responsibility for specific production areas.

It's not enough to identify the jobs to be done and break them into component parts. To get back on track a team must also address any problems in skill competency among its members. Are all team members cross-trained in the critical functions of the team? Where do gaps exist that affect team results?

Building Skill Competencies

Skill competencies can be divided into two areas: technical skills and behavioral skills. Here is a step-by-step process that a team can use for building and reviewing competencies:

1. Identify specific team tasks or responsibilities (the team or management can do this). Tasks might include any of the following:

- Sign work orders.
- Schedule vacations.
- Determine and plan for overtime.
- Call for maintenance help.
- Complete reports.
- Intervene on customer's behalf.
- Troubleshoot equipment.
- Determine absence coverage.
- Prioritize work.
- Schedule and carry out changeovers.
- Maintain area records and documentation.
- Assign workers to jobs.
- Purchase supplies and equipment.
- Suggest and implement improvements.
- Train new employees.
- Plan and lead meetings.
- Coordinate workflow.
- Call for assistance when needed.
- Solve problems when they arise.
- Make exceptions to procedures.
- Coordinate special project or event.
- Replace merchandise.
- Refund money and authorize credit.
- Rework product/service.
- Monitor safety.
- Perform account reconciliations.
- Provide and prepare budgets.
- Respond to internal and external customer complaints.
- Set team goals.
- Work with external customers and suppliers.
- Select work methods.
- Maintain housekeeping.
- Monitor and control costs.
- Stop work in progress to address quality issues.

• Recognize and reward members.
• Make compensation decisions.

2. Identify what percentage of the task the team is currently doing and what percentage is being done by someone else (management or supervisors). If the team is already doing almost all of the task, it will be easier for the team to take on the task than if it is a task that they have never done before. (See Figure 2-1.)

3. Divide the task list into four phases on the basis of the level of competency required. The level is determined by the current competency of the team to perform the task and the amount of responsibility or authority required. This is a much better approach than arbitrarily deciding that a team should do a task in year two or three.

4. Identify and describe what is needed to perform specific technical and behavioral tasks, ranging from work orders and scheduling to budgeting and team reviews. The team determines the key skills needed and the level of responsibility. (See examples later in this section.)

5. Once the competencies are established for the given task, decide what is needed to bring the team to an acceptable level in order for the task to be transferred (Figures 2-2 and 2-3).

Figure 2-1. Sample delegation grid.

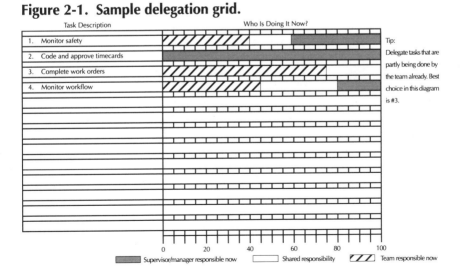

Figure 2-2. Technical skill competency assessment.

Task: _Signing work orders_

Category	What Do They Need to Know How to Do?	What Do They Need to Be Taught?
A. _Job knowledge_ Has the skills, knowledge, and ability to complete task according to accepted procedure	Follow procedure Know codes Use equipment Who has the authority to sign Set priorities	How to determine different priority levels
B. _Productivity_ Meets standard output; efficiency and follow-through; timeliness	Fit work order within work schedule Follow up if no response	Follow-up procedure
C. _Quality of work_ Meets accuracy, reliability, and appearance standards	Discuss problem accurately Complete form accurately Write legibly Complete instructions or attachments to explain problem fully	How to complete form
D. _Communication skills_ Communicates clearly and effectively about task, both orally and in writing	Describe problem Describe status of equipment Stress urgency/need	

E. *Equipment* Uses equipment properly and observes all safety provisions	Understand equipment Know equipment Understand flow patterns Understand effect problem has on production Follow contamination procedure Follow safety rules Know lock-out procedure	Review lock-out procedure
F. *Environmental* Understands relevant customer policies, restrictions, etc.	Interface with maintenance	How to respond to maintenance issues

6. Summarize the team's ability to take on the task by reviewing the overall skill and behavior competencies and then asking the following:

- How have we responded to similar tasks in the past?
- To what degree have we initiated or been requested to do this task?
- To what degree does the task correspond to past or present organizational practices?

7. Develops an action plan that identifies each competency to be mastered, how it will be done, and by when.

Determining Competencies

Although the process of analyzing competencies may seem time-consuming, there is tremendous value in breaking down a task

Figure 2-3. Behavioral skill competency assessment.

Task: _Signing work orders_

Category	What Do They Need to Know How to Do?	What Do They Need to Be Taught?
A. *Interpersonal skills* Is responsive to others; is cooperative; promotes unity	Resolve shift-to-shift conflict Listen effectively	Conflict-resolution skills
B. *Dependability* Is prompt; complies with work procedures; is reliable	Anticipate need for and initiate improvement Self-start Assume responsibility for work order	
C. *Adaptability and flexibility* Adjusts to change	Make good decisions Have a flexible attitude	How to review decision criteria
D. *Managing Workload* Organizes, plans, and prioritizes	Know what to do first Handle pressure well Deal with conflicting priorities	How items are classified Procedure for handling priority conflicts
E. *Responsibility* Is self-starting; takes initiative; is open-minded	Identify problems Suggest solutions Take action Have self-esteem	

F. Responsiveness to authority Follows instruction; supports authority	Be able and willing to follow recommended procedure	Levels of authority
G. Acceptance of suggestions and criticism	*Give and get feedback*	*Feedback guidelines*
H. Creativity and risk taking	*Recognize what constitutes a risk.*	*Risk-taking procedure*

into identifiable competencies. This series of questions can guide a team in the process.

Identifying Technical Competencies

- *Job knowledge.* What skills, knowledge, and abilities are needed to complete the task according to current accepted procedure?
- *Productivity.* What abilities are needed to meet standard output, efficiency, and follow-through?
- *Quality of work.* What abilities are needed to meet accuracy, reliability, and appearance standards?
- *Communication skills.* What abilities are needed to communicate clearly and effectively, both verbally and in writing, about the task?
- *Equipment.* What abilities are required to use equipment properly and to observe all safety provisions?
- *Environment.* What level of understanding is needed to comply with all relevant customer policies, restrictions, OSHA requirements, and personnel policies?

Identifying Behavioral Competencies

- *Interpersonal skills.* What competencies are required regarding responsiveness to others, including listening and speaking?

• *Dependability.* What abilities are needed to be prompt and reliable, and to comply with work procedures?
• *Adaptability and flexibility.* What competencies are needed to adjust to constant change?
• *Managing workload.* What abilities are needed to organize, plan, and prioritize work and to handle pressure?
• *Responsibility.* What competencies are required to take initiative and to be open-minded and self-starting?
• *Responsiveness to authority.* What abilities are needed to follow procedure and instruction and to support the team's designated authorities (e.g., team leader, team decisions)?
• *Acceptance of suggestions and criticisms.* What abilities are required to give and receive feedback?
• *Creativity and risk taking.* What strategies can be used to encourage and develop creativity and risk taking?

Clearly there is a connection between a real or perceived lack of competency and team member resistance. When people do not believe they can be successful, they will thwart the process.

Handling Recurring Resistance

Getting back on track often means handling a new wave of resistance that occurs as the team presses to address disconnections, competency issues, and role clarity. It is important to review the cycle of involvement (see Chapter 1), understand the reasons for the resistance at this point, and identify the stages in the resistance pattern. When in doubt, remember to go back to awareness and increase the level of understanding.

Reasons for Mid-Stage Resistance

• The original goal, purpose, or vision is lost.
• Anticipation is building that real behavior change will be required.
• The pain associated with change is being felt among members.
• Loyalty to routine and particular approaches is great.

- Compounding multiple fears are developing as the press to change behavior escalates.
- Stress related to rapid change and feelings of lack of control increases.

Four Stages in the Resistance Pattern

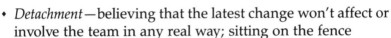

Stage 1. Team member responds with suspicion, uncertainty, and obstinacy. The symptoms of this type of resistance include:

- *Detachment*—believing that the latest change won't affect or involve the team in any real way; sitting on the fence
- *Agreement without commitment*—going along but not matching verbal comments with supportive behavior
- *Delay*—clinging to what is known and seems to work; being reluctant to give it up; withholding support but not working against the change
- *Moaning and groaning*—complaining about the change; attempting to gather support for negative viewpoint
- *Defiance*—looking for ways to prevent or sabotage the improvements, either directly or indirectly, because the team is convinced the improvements won't really work; finger-pointing and blaming
- *Passive resistance*—making covert attempts to block improvements by denying responsibility for nonsupport

Stage 2. The team member begins to have a growing realization of the positive possibilities of the improvement strategies. The team member is willing to recognize that something good might come out of the change.

A workshop participant was having considerable difficulty with the concept of empowerment until his son had a problem in school one day. The participant ended up using some of the coaching skills he had learned in training to help his son and came into training the next day with a very different attitude.

Stage 3. The team member demonstrates a willingness to examine old roles and to explore new ones with a "think yes before no" attitude. Ironically, the team member now seems impatient to get started, acting as if someone else has been responsible for holding things back.

Stage 4. The team member shows a willingness to learn the new approach and terminology. The resistance has subsided.

Certainly many readers will say, "On what planet does resistance to change ever resolve itself as smoothly as that?" Stage One resistance, ranging from detachment to defiance, can go on for many months. Ultimately, however, people either show signs of adapting or begin to leave. It is not unusual for between 15 and 25 percent of the organization to be struggling at any one time with the use of teams.

Adapting to Rapid Change

As one mid-sized manufacturing company was launching its move to self-directed work teams, it was also going through the largest expansion in its history and was a "sold-out" plant (that is, it was operating at maximum production capacity). There was every reason for the team initiative to fall apart under the pressure of change. More than anything else, the strong commitment of plant management was the glue that held it together.

All teams today face constant change. Customer demands and new technology can cause disruption on a regular basis. Teams in the middle years don't get the same amount of attention they did in the early days, so they often feel left on their own to deal with change. Recognizing the stages of change can help the team to adapt more smoothly.

The Stages of Change

Change can be divided into four stages: visioning, planning, action, and follow-through. The team's ability to adapt to constant change will be improved if at each stage it follows these steps:

1. *Vision stage:* Create a dynamic vision of the future.

- Involve the team in the vision development. Choose to co-create the vision with others in the organization, department, or team.

- Anticipate the impact of the changes, and set realistic goals.
- Be bold, yet emphasize stability.
- Mix up key players, and invite new blood into the teams.
- Communicate clearly about expectations; be realistic about estimating the levels of resistance.

2. *Planning stage:* Develop a plan for the new changes.

- Schedule the change plan with specific milestones.
- Check structure, systems, culture, and capabilities.
- Create a change team; involve the resistant.
- Simulate the new environment; consider a pilot effort.

3. *Action stage:* Determine actions to be taken.

- Involve the team in designing the action plan.
- Provide information; give orientation and training.
- Establish new routines.
- Develop a tracking system for monitoring and updating.
- Build a support system and create job aids.
- Communicate constantly; give generous feedback on progress.
- Celebrate every success; mark every milestone.

4. *Follow-through stage:* Promote continuous improvement.

- Evaluate effectiveness of the change.
- Monitor climate and attitude.
- Check progress against benchmarks.
- Emphasize the new way.
- Document and communicate improvements.

Situations may occur that are outside of the team's control, sometimes just as the team is getting back on track and addressing change issues. Layoffs and downsizing, for example, can be devastating for teams.

Recovering From Losses Associated With Layoffs and Downsizing

There is a common myth among teams that no team member will ever lose his or her job. The myth is founded on the misguided assumptions that members will cover over performance problems for each other and organizations with teams are kinder and gentler on performance than traditional organizations are. The reality is quite different. Members of a team that has lost two or three members need to spend time processing the loss, assessing the impact on and the changes required of the team, and deciding whether to recommit to what will be a "new" team.

Shortly after training was completed for teams in a lubricating systems company, the organization eliminated ten positions. All the trust that had been built during the training sessions went back to zero. Some members worried that they might be next, causing a return to "every man for himself" thinking. Others said, "Forget about doing this team thing; I just want to keep my job." There is no magic bullet that will eliminate the damage of layoffs and downsizing. However, there are some remedies to ease the pain and speed the return to normalcy:

- Top-level management must show visible involvement in the "newly reformed" organization and teams and encourage and involve the teams in devising strategy and designing the changes.
- Consider identifying a communications coordinator to keep teams informed and gather employee feedback, including ideas, questions, and gripes. Explain exactly why and how the downsizing occurred. The deeper and broader the cuts, the greater the need for ongoing communication to deal with the threatening aspects of the change.
- Don't prolong the process any more than is absolutely necessary. Reduction in force should be done quickly to prevent uncertainty, insecurity, disruption, paralysis, and panic.
- Select and train a coaching task force to oversee retraining, new job assignments, and work-sharing (see Chapter 8) for the people who remain.

- Provide extra training to prepare employees for new responsibilities.
- Make career paths more horizontal and more interesting.
- Recognize that layoffs and downsizing profoundly affect everyone involved. Be responsive to the aftershocks, including low morale, fear of future cutbacks, declining productivity, and mistrust of management. Work hard to recreate loyalty and trust.

QUESTIONS AND ANSWERS:
Getting Back on Track

1. **Q.** *Our self-directed team developed a sample goal early in its training process with the assistance of the trainer. Now the training is complete, but the team seems to be directionless. What can we do?*

   A. A number of questions need to be answered first: Is the goal still relevant? Did the team ever buy into the goal to begin with or was it just a training exercise? Do team members plan to reexamine the goal, and do they know how to do it? It's common to set goals in the beginning and then never refine or revisit them. It makes sense for every team to reexamine goals and direction at least every six months.

2. **Q.** *Our team is struggling with how best to work with our former supervisor. Some team members still defer to this person's judgment; they even stop generating ideas the minute he comes into the room. Others seem to get combative and suggest things that don't make sense just to make a statement of independence. The supervisor has trouble when he sees the error in judgment and usually steps in to correct the problem.*

   A. Supervisors have by far the most difficult transition in the team environment. They often feel that people are saying that everything they have done in the past is wrong. It's best to acknowledge that roles are in transition. The team and the supervisor need to sit down periodically and talk about how things are going. This works well if the team members can be candid, yet kind. If people are angry, then the role discussions should take on more of a negotiation flavor, with an impartial facilitator helping participants articulate and work through their differences.

3. **Q.** *Many of the team members have very bad memories of school. They didn't show much interest in applying the training and being a team. How will we ever get them interested in training again?*

   A. Training needs to occur in the team environment. Every month or so it pays to have new or refresher training on some aspect of group process. The norm is for teams to have considerable preliminary training and then go on their own. However, the new skills that members have acquired will not last if they are not reinforced. The more the team can be involved in identifying its own training needs and the content it sees as relevant, the more receptive it will be to training. Learner-directed training is very popular with teams.

4. **Q.** *One person does not like the idea of teams. He's been with the company for a long time and sees no need to use teams. He constantly puts down the work of the team and any member who tries to make the team concept work. The team is at the boiling point and has asked management to intervene.*

   A. I'd ask first whether any team members have spoken to this person directly and shared feedback. On a more general approach, the organization needs to begin to modify its performance measures and compensation decisions to reflect the importance of teams. As this person experiences the consequences of not changing, he may suddenly see the light when it begins to affect his paycheck or job security. Change won't happen if it's made optional.

5. **Q.** *We've been using teams for almost two years, and even though we rotated the team jobs in the beginning, now most of the jobs are being done by four or five team members. The rest are doing things the same way they always have. The*

*more responsible members are now saying that they won't
do any more for the team until others start to help.*

A. I'd be inclined to gather data on the tasks to be completed,
the competencies required, and who is currently doing what.
These data should make clear who is doing it all and who
isn't contributing. Then I'd set up a training program to teach
or retrain those who aren't contributing and provide some
incentives (skill-based pay, for example) to motivate them to
want to learn and use their new skills. Focus on the system
(the what) instead of the people (the who), and see if that
makes a difference.

6. **Q.** *The jealousy between two teams has existed since the beginning. One team won the favor of management early on because it was so eager. When the teams have to work together,
the level of trust is nonexistent. During a joint meeting recently, each of the teams sat on opposite sides of the room
and spent most of the time blaming each other for the break-
down in communication.*

A. It strikes me that these two teams need a common goal, a
divided-up task list, and deadlines, rather than more rhetoric
about the importance of getting along. Sometimes the very
act of getting people focused on a specific task or project can
help overcome disagreements and differences.

7. **Q.** *Is it unrealistic to think we can achieve the transformation to
teams during these times of intense change?*

A. I don't really see that an organization has much choice. The
future is pressing in, and we all must be able to achieve more
with the human resources we have. I recently led the top
management of an organization through a four-module series of training on teams and total quality management so
that the company could decide whether to proceed with a
culture change. Each person agreed at the end that change
was absolutely necessary if the company expected to stay
competitive. But when we asked who would be willing to
champion the process, no one volunteered. The reason: no

one had enough time. Putting out fires was so time-consuming that fire prevention was an impossibility. The company just gave its competition a window of time to get ahead.

8. **Q.** *What if our team leaders do not have extensive task expertise?*

    A. Typically the team leader role is an administrative function. It usually takes a team leader in a self-directed work team three to four passes through the position to feel confident in the job. Leaders don't need to know how to do every job on the team, but they do need to have good team members who provide honest information. There is no reason why a team leader can't ask a team member to join in a discussion with an engineer, for example, if the team leader doesn't know all the answers.

9. **Q.** *How should we handle our approach to teams when we see things that need correcting?*

    A. Many managers and supervisors suddenly become very timid about surfacing problems with a team for fear that someone will accuse them of being nonsupportive and uncooperative. In truth, one of the key responsibilities of managers and supervisors is to point out where problems may be occurring and to coach and guide the team through a correction process. Tone of voice and attitude are critically important here. If a manager has been just waiting for a team to make a mistake and then pounces, her effort will backfire. However, a manager who stays focused on the problem and reinforces the point that the people on the team are important contributors for solving the problem will do fine.

10. **Q.** *Is the team leader's effectiveness influenced by the climate and culture in the organization?*

    A. Absolutely! A team leader is constantly interacting with other teams, department managers, staff, suppliers, and customers. If morale is bad, it will influence how collaborative people are willing to be with each other. Poor communication, low trust, and territorialism will all impact the team leader's success. If the culture doesn't fully support teams yet, the leader's interactions with department managers and professional staff will be difficult. People outside the team can be very critical and make snide and cutting remarks to team members. Although the behavior is caused by insecurity, it doesn't help the team member who's the brunt of an outside attack.

Note

1. R. Guzzo and E. Salas and associates, *Team Effectiveness and Decision Making in Organizations* (San Francisco: Jossey-Bass, 1995).

3
Keeping It Fresh

Somewhere around three years into the transition to self-directed teams, teams often ask again, "Why *are* we doing this?" The benefits are overlooked. The initial excitement of becoming a team is gone; the hoopla has been replaced with more work and more responsibility. Nobody's paying any attention to the team anymore. The "drifting away" is beginning to occur. It's time to review the specific benefits of being a team, including:

* Increased productivity and performance capability
* Improved morale through enhanced dignity, self-esteem, and job satisfaction
* Greater participation in hiring, safety, process changes, improvements, and training
* Increased ability and desire to improve
* More ownership and involvement of employees in redesign
* Better perspective on the whole job
* Better understanding of how to make improvements
* Better coverage during emergency and overtime situations
* Greater appreciation of others' work
* Increased communication between management and other employees
* Fewer layers of supervision
* More control over work life and therefore less stress

Most teams begin with team-building training that lasts for several months. The team then goes to work on the project or task, and the training stops. A year later the team reverts to many of its old behaviors, and people don't understand why. Keeping the team fresh requires that management identify ways to recycle information and commitment back to the team on a regular basis. Yet continual training is a major effort often rejected by both management and team members. They lament, "People are tired of training. They know this stuff already." The goal must therefore be a self-sustaining system of renewal. New behavior cannot win against instilled, old behavior that is constantly being reinforced.

This chapter explores various types of renewal efforts for the team, ranging from a large-scale renewal plan to team-specific measures such as ongoing training, improved team meetings, and membership changes. Like any process, team building should include a wide range of activities designed to keep the team fresh and vibrant. The mistake is to assume that teamwork requires little or no effort once the team is established.

Sequential Development Needs of Teams

Teams have very specific developmental needs that must be taught as the teams mature. The work of renewal may require revisiting this list time and time again.

Developmental Needs of Teams

- General statement of and commitment to a common goal
- General acknowledgment of the interdependence of team members as they work to accomplish the goal
- Ability to perform simple roles (scribe, timekeeper)
- Expansion of the capability of the team facilitation
- Development of help/hinder list
- Description and assignment of process observer role
- Description and assignment of team leader role (the ongoing contact point person for the team)
- Use of team-oriented meeting skills (developing and agreeing on an agenda, allocating time as a team, deciding what to do with leftover agenda items, deciding what to do when an agenda item runs over allotted time)
- Development of team norms for handling issues such as: attendance, punctuality, confidentiality, duration and fre-

quency of meetings, guests, team records, subgrouping, authority/boundaries, new members, and interteam relationship issues (each team will have its own set of norms and may need to revisit these from time to time)

* Development of team problem-solving skills, including knowledge of how to use the following skills: brainstorming/brainwriting, multivoting, affinity diagrams, nominal group technique, flowcharting, data gathering including Paretos and fishbones, tree diagrams, implication wheels, relationship diagrams, decision matrix, and reengineering process analysis
* Development of ability to achieve consensus decisions; clarity about when to use consensus, the steps in building consensus decisions, attitudes required to reach consensus, blocking and using stand-asides
* Understanding of group dynamics including groupthink, Abilene paradox, group tyranny, collective rationalization, negative stereotyping, and pressure for self-censorship
* Skill development in conflict resolution, including setting up a team method for handling disagreements or behavior problems, learning to appreciate differences, understanding the importance of trust and what builds or breaks down trust
* Development of team rewards and recognition, including how to recognize individual achievement while maintaining team spirit and how to set up effective measures for teams, and of strategies to celebrate success

The Renewal Process

Team renewal is an onging process that can involve team members, management, and even customers. Nothing is more important to a team in the middle years than having a process for reaffirming the value of its existence. This process can be a part of regular team meetings or it can be disguised as a refresher retreat. To encourage renewal:

- Establish and maintain buy-in by regularly identifying the costs and benefits of teams. If productivity has surpassed preteam levels, announce it to everyone.
- Review roles and expectations on a regular basis, especially if turnover occurs. Role definition needs to exist for team members, management, leadership positions, and support groups. Expand the role relationships to include customers and suppliers.
- Develop measures of performance for both the hard and the soft skills. Report on the measures regularly. Keep an active scoreboard.
- Develop a two-way performance feedback system that encourages regular praise and constructive criticism.
- Establish a system of accountability. Discourage caretaking and overfunctioning on the part of managers and supervisors.
- Implement a recognition system that promotes and rewards teams.
- Establish guidelines for leadership that put more emphasis on mentoring and coaching than on commanding and controlling.
- Define an ongoing training program that is based on needs identified by the team. Let the team develop its own training plan.
- Review and revise measurement tools and systems.
- Determine new methods for handling discipline problems.
- Handoff higher-level tasks by using hiring teams and in-house trainers to do the work.
- Focus on continuous improvement of team meetings and team decision making.

> Q&A
> #2

> Q&A
> #4

A pediatric nursing team lost most of its steam eighteen months into the process. Members had made major strides toward improving unit productivity, scheduling, and patient care—even their relationships with physicians and the lab. Renewal for them meant addressing their feelings of plateauing and then identifying some new, short-term, challenging goals.

The Team Renewal Plan

When teams experience what is called "plateauing," this approach can break the malaise:

1. Call for volunteers to participate in a task force to design a renewal plan for the team. If possible, seek complete representation of processes, functions, and levels in the department. Include more nonsupervisors than supervisors, and look for people who have ideas for improvement as well as concerns about the current process.
2. Determine the key problems, and define the parameters of the renewal process (cost, time, quantity).
3. Meet regularly to design a system of renewal. Use subgroups (as previously discussed) to work on discrete issues such as format and training.
4. Regularly solicit opinions of others by asking, "Do you like how the renewal plan is shaping up? What do you like about it?"
5. Research the best systems by benchmarking with other companies. Encourage team members to attend conferences and present their results to others or to join a local quality consortium to share ideas.
6. Finalize the renewal plan. Name it.
7. Increase the amount of communication fourfold.
8. Define objectives by linking them to business strategies. Ask questions such as "Where are we going?" "What will it look like when we get there?" "How will we get there?" and "How will we handle things differently?" Measure the objectives with time limits, productivity groups, and/or desired outcomes.
9. Create a plan of action. Assign ownership of action items. Develop a timeline.
10. Measure and evaluate as the renewal plan is implemented. Hold follow-up discussions to be certain members feel energized.

Sometimes it's helpful to encourage team members to attend presentations on teams, quality, customer satisfaction, or other relevant topics. They can bring back ideas to share with the other members of the team. Organizations often send whole contingents of teams to conferences to give presentations and to participate in the workshops. At the end of each day, the teams debrief each other, sharing the best ideas from all the sessions.

The renewal plan needs to be developed at the end of the first year and reexamined by the team every six months thereafter. One option is to submit the renewal plan to the resource team (or oversight team) that authorizes the plan and budget.

Strategies for Refreshing Teams

Organizations can use a number of techniques to try to breathe new life into plateauing teams.

Implementing Effective Team Training

Training is the technique most commonly used to revitalize the team and those who affect it. The training should focus on both the theoretical and the practical. Many participants want to focus on the concrete, but the training units should develop an understanding of the philosophy underpinning the use of teams that they can use in all future decision making. The proverb "Give me a fish and I'll eat for a day; teach me to fish and I'll fish for a lifetime" is apt in this situation.

There is much discussion about whether training should be done "just when it's needed" or whether organizations need to take preventive steps, preparing the team to handle anything that might happen (e.g., whether conflict resolution training should occur only after a conflict has emerged or before any conflict has surfaced). Here are some insights into team-building training:

1. Teams do well when early training focuses on specific "how tos" such as running a meeting, being a team leader, creating the hand-off plan.
2. Teams do not always respond well to abstract team-building activities such as hypothetical survival games. While they may enjoy the training, they often have difficulty re-

lating it to the actual functioning of the team. Over time, having too many games frustrate team members.

3. Intense skill development such as training in facilitation and conflict mediation are better done in laboratory sessions where participants actually hold a meeting or discuss a conflict and training occurs as the activity evolves. The trainer conducts "stop-action" skill building and then encourages the participants to put new skills into practice on the spot.

4. The more mature the team, the less its tolerance for canned presentations. Mature teams typically want experienced trainers who respond well to challenging statements and questions. Trainers who tightly control their sessions or who project a "know-it-all" attitude do not do well with experienced teams.

5. There seems to be a limit to the amount of training teams can absorb before needing a break. Typically, six to eight training modules every other week is the limit. Then it's best to give the team a break and return to training after a couple of months.

Q&A #5

Q&A #6

Ground Rules for Effective Team Training

1. Allow, expect, and encourage participation.
2. Incorporate all ideas and experiences to enrich the training.
3. Start and end sessions on time.
4. Have participants turn off pagers or leave them outside the training room.
5. Use trainers as a resource and have them available before and after training and during breaks to answer questions.
6. Encourage and expect questions.
7. Give homework assignments after each session.
8. Require that participants who miss sessions assume responsibility for picking up new training materials and reviewing the training (and videotapes) with one of the in-house trainers.
9. Allow breaks to discourage interruptions and participants' coming in and going out during the training.

10. Allow participants to share general information about the training outside the session but not to refer to specific individuals or situations.

Twenty-Five Sample Core Training Units

Team training topics typically fall into six categories, ranging from developing a general understanding of teams to managing team tasks. Each category contains a number of subtopics that are particularly important for skill development; there is a total of twenty-five core training units.

Keeping the team fresh can involve either providing reviews of the core units or, if appropriate, recognizing that a core unit was never completed and filling the gap.

We have found that these twenty-five core units form the heart of team training. They are shown in lettered lists in the following outline:

1. Understanding Teams
   a. History of Teams
   b. Types of Teams and Their Unique Roles
   c. Team Values and Vision
2. Launching the Team
   a. Defining Purpose and Goals
   b. Reviewing the Team Charter
   c. Setting Up and Managing Better Team Meetings
3. Understanding Team Roles
   a. Understanding Various Roles on a Team
   b. Improving the Role of Team Leader
   c. Building Facilitation Skills
   d. Interacting with Others Outside the Team
   e. Management's Role as Coach
4. Building Team Relationships
   a. Building Trust on the Team
   b. Renewing Team Ground Rules
   c. Gaining Support and Participation from Important Others
   d. Communication Styles
   e. Giving and Getting Better Feedback

    f. Developing Interpersonal Skills
    g. Conflict Resolution Strategies for Teams
    h. More Team Problem-Solving Tools
    i. Improving Consensus Decision Making
5. Managing Team Tasks
    a. Taking On More Responsibility and Accountability
    b. Analyzing Work Processes
    c. Measuring Results
6. Realizing Rewards and Recognition
    a. Intrinsic and Extrinsic Team Rewards
    b. Adapting the Organization's Systems (Compensation and Evaluation) to Teams

Identifying New Team Goals

Refreshing the team can also be done with the development of new, exciting goals that focus on key outputs such as quality, customer satisfaction, cost, and delivery. Steps to team goal setting include:

1. Review of the organization's mission, vision, and values and of the department's business unit plan.
2. Identification of new opportunities created by the organization's plan, including high-leverage opportunities where performance is low and it is easy to make opportunities.
3. Identification of constraints that will negatively affect good opportunities (e.g., cost, phaseout, and staff reductions).
4. Determination of customer needs, including team visits with customers to gather information and see how the company's product or service is being used.
5. Development of goal statements that are SMART (specific, measurable, achievable, results-oriented, and time-bound).
6. Creation of standards for measuring goal achievement in a precise manner.
7. Prioritization of goals to identify the top three or four goals. Analyze the goals on the basis of their contribution

to the organization's objectives, potential for improving customer satisfaction, and relative importance to other goals.

One of the fundamental characteristics of a team, unlike a committee, is the development of a common goal and the recognition of team members' interdependence. Yet most teams do not use goal setting as effectively as they could. Goal setting should occur:

- At every meeting as the team discusses various agenda items. The phrase "What is our goal here?" should be a frequently heard one.
- Whenever the team is lost and discussion has been going around in circles and going nowhere.
- Whenever the team is polarized over a specific strategy or plan and is losing sight of the big picture.
- Every four to six months for project-specific team goals. Part of a team meeting should be reserved for discussion of the question "What are we trying to accomplish with this project?"
- Annually to be certain the team's overall goals are in alignment with the organization's goals. This goal-setting session should include members of management, who openly discuss the organization's direction.

Typical Problems With Goal Setting

- Members have never done goal setting before and need help getting started and achieving consensus.
- Goal statements are too big and broad, and team members soon lose interst in ever hoping to accomplish the goal.
- Members fear that they may not be able to accomplish the goal and wonder how management will respond. They need encouragement and support to overcome the fear.
- Nothing happens when the goal is reached, except for more work on some other project. Goal attainment must be celebrated for goal setting to work.
- People quickly digress into defining how to achieve the

goal (tactical solutions) rather than working to clarify all the components of the goal.
- People who are "doers" resist the planning nature of goal setting and just want to get started. They fail to realize that getting started without a common goal will send the team off in countless different directions.

Improving Meeting Processes

Effective team goal setting dramatically improves another team function that often needs refreshing: team meetings. During a visit to an organization, we were invited to sit in on a customer service team meeting to observe and offer suggestions. The customer service team was two years old and had been through team training in its first year. We observed the following problems:

- The team did not have an agenda. The facilitator simply said, "What do we want to talk about today?" and then the team spent ten minutes of the meeting time deciding. Time was not allocated for each agenda item, so only a few of the items ended up being discussed.

- The focus of the meeting was on information sharing rather than on planning and problem solving. Because of the focus on information, people spent more time listening to reports than on interacting and utilizing the brainpower in the room. People began to fade and tune out as members shared the same information over and over.

- No one really asked the facilitator for permission to speak. Members just jumped in in the middle of someone else's comment. Twice during the meeting side conversations distracted attention from the person who was speaking. No one functioned as process observer.

- As the team discussed whether to begin cross-training on various accounts, one member suggested voting on the idea. The facilitator did not encourage the team to press for consensus. Instead he called for a vote; the team split five to three not to begin the training.

- When time was up the meeting ended, and everyone left.

Most participants described it as a fairly typical meeting for the customer service team.

Suggestions for Improving Team Meetings

• The team develops an agenda. Every meeting should have a goal (what the team wants to accomplish) and an agenda ("the things to be done" in Latin). A clipboard with a blank agenda sheet can be hung up during the week for members to list agenda items (see Figure 3-1). As they identify agenda items, members should indicate the time requirement, the priority of the item, and who will be presenting the topic to the team.

• The facilitator reviews the items listed on the agenda sheet, puts them in tentative priority order, and distributes the agenda (with time frames and presenters) to all members before the meeting. If items on the agenda are informational only, the facilitator discusses with the person the possibility of sharing the information in another format (memo, E-mail, handout at the meeting).

• The meeting opens on time with housekeeping details, including selection of scribe, timekeeper, and process observer. The process observer is responsible for surfacing any behaviors that are hindering team effectiveness. These behaviors have been identified early in the team's development and put on a help/hinder list that the process observer has at the meeting.

• The facilitator reviews the agenda items and gets team agreement on the items and their order. New items are added and time reallocated as needed.

• The team proceeds through its items, encouraging full team discussion. Brainstorming is a common occurrence. The facilitator encourages those members who are not speaking to join in.

• The timekeeper gives a five-minute warning before the end of each discussion item and lets the team know when discussion time is up. The team members then decide whether to give the item more time and, if so, what item will be given reduced time or eliminated from the agenda. This decision is made by the team, not by the facilitator.

- As the discussion narrows to a decision point, the facilitator listens for areas of agreement among the team members and poses these as points of possible consensus. The team votes only to narrow the choices (multivoting and Nominal Group Technique as outlined in my book, *The Team Building Tool Kit*), never to reach a final decision. Members indicate their agreement with a nod of the head or some other consensus indicator (see Chapter 6).
- The facilitator proceeds with follow-up on the decision item by asking for volunteers to own various action items. The scribe records all the action items on a separate list (see Figure 3-2) that is read by the scribe at the close of the meeting so that all members are reminded about the tasks they have agreed to do. If the scribe writes up minutes, the minutes should list action items separately, as well as carryover agenda items.
- The facilitator asks the scribe to read the action items and the new agenda items that have resulted from the discussion. Agenda items that were tabled or not dealt with because of time constraints are noted, and the facilitator asks the team members what they would like to do with these items. The team reaches a consensus decision.
- The meeting ends on time with all members clear about what items have been discussed, what decisions have been made, who is responsible for doing what action items, and how leftover items are being handled.
- The date, time, and location of the next meeting are determined.

A maturing team could easily take each of these steps apart and refresh its meetings by evaluating how it is currently handling each item and developing improvement strategies. Teams should also explore how to use all types of problem-solving and decision-making tools (see Chapter 6) to improve the team dynamics. If a team is simply presenting items for discussion and then debating back and forth on the basis of personal opinion, the team is not operating at an acceptable level of meeting performance.

Figure 3-1. Agenda preparation.

Agenda Item	Presenter	Priority (1 = high)	Time Needed	Special Notes
Problem with a cellular team	Janice	1+	15 min.	
Team trip to supplier	Bob	2	10 min.	Handout
Arrival of new equipment	Sam	1	15 min.	Need planning time

Figure 3-2. Action items.

Team

Meeting Date

Topic	Action Item(s)	Person(s) Responsible	Deadline Date	Special Notes
Planning agenda for joint team meeting	Invite other team	Lynn		
	Distribute materials	Joan		
	Prepare how team will discuss problem	Jerry		
	Create agenda	Tom		

Using Outsiders to Refresh the Team

Sometimes teams begin to fade because of familiarity; it's always the same people saying the same things. If this is the case, the team will benefit from the introduction of some new people, either as team members or as liaisons to other teams. During the second and third levels of team development (what researchers have called the storming or argumentative stage and the norming or rule-setting stage), however, teams often resist adding new members or letting outsiders in. It's as if they have come to know each other's quirks and have no desire to alter the group dynamic. This tendency recedes by the fourth level of team development (the performing stage, when goals and roles are clear and supported), when the team is actually eager to share ideas and listen to outsiders. However, teams can be dramatically refreshed by visiting with, listening to, and sharing stories with other people and teams, both inside and outside their own organization. Management needs to strongly encourage this process of reaching out to others.

Benchmarking With Other Teams

- Try to identify teams from comparable organizations in terms of size, length of time in the team-building process, and work processes. If the teams' work environments are too different, teams have a tendency to rule out each other's experience as being "unlike our own."
- Recognize the tendency to critique and compare what other teams are doing and structure a postvisit discussion to include both the pros and cons of alternate ways of operating.
- Encourage as much team-to-team discussion (with minimal management intervention) as possible.
- Try to establish ongoing relationships with other organizations in which mutual sharing is a periodic activity (occurring every six months or so). Videotaping meetings or special events (picnics, team celebrations) is an effective way to keep teams in touch with one another.

Using New Technology

One of the most effective ways to keep team members and separate teams in touch with one another is through the use of new technology. Teams can take advantage of the technology to refresh their attitudes. Teams and/or team members who work in geographically separate locations can benefit tremendously from new technology, including electronic mail, the Internet, conference calling, answering machines, car phones, modems, fax machines, and interactive television. Very often a new "toy"—even one as simple as a team answering machine—can refresh the team's spirit.

An organization with teams in two different states regularly holds meetings and training sessions in which one team hosts the session via a conference call and the other team listens in. Sessions are videotaped, and a fax machine enables the teams to share material instantly. The next time the location is reversed, so neither team is favored. Most important, both teams work hard to make the technology work for them. Another team in a sales department connects with its sister team via E-mail and car phones. Most important here, organizations need to be receptive to exploring how new technologies can be used to enhance team effectiveness.

Handling Job Sharing

One of the characteristics of a well-functioning team is its members' ability to switch or share jobs. Job sharing can add variety to team member jobs and strengthen the overall functioning of the team. However, job sharing is not always easy to bring about. Melvin Blumberg[1] in his research with job switching in a Pennsylvania mine makes some important points about job sharing:

* Teams are best able to self-manage where members are multiskilled.
* The more jobs are switched among all team members, the more status difference is reduced.
* Improved communication and greater stability in the internal structure exists when job sharing is practiced.

- Individuals who have spent years accumulating job skills tend to resist changes that will make their years of experience obsolete.
- Early nonrewarding or punishing experiences with learning situations diminish members' interest in new learning situations.
- Members often believe that knowing how to perform an undesirable job will lead to their being assigned to that job permanently.
- Job sharing occurs more readily when special rewards to any job classification are avoided.
- There is a positive correlation between a member's willingness to job-switch and her level of education and attitude.
- There is a negative correlation between willingness to job-switch and seniority and age.
- Any piece-incentive system discourages effective job sharing.

A cellular manufacturing team found members very resistant to job sharing as long as the organization maintained its traditional piece-incentive pay system. The team had a best "molder" and "grinder" and saw no reason to put less skilled people on those jobs, especially when their inability to maintain output affected the team's total pay. As much as management structured the team roles to rotate in the beginning, it didn't take long for the teams to shift to the more traditional system. The organization continues to have difficulty with this and will until it changes its compensation system.

Tips for Job Sharing

- Encourage the team to identify the five or six job tasks that are critical to the success of the team. Assess each team member's ability to perform those tasks. If any members are weak, proceed with job-sharing training.

- Establish a standardized process for completing the task. Reengineer the process before inaugurating job sharing so that the most efficient and effective process is used. Flowchart the process and identify any allowable variations in procedure. Write up standardized procedures and make them available to all team members.

♦ Identify very specific skills to be accomplished at each step in the training. Identify how skill accomplishment will be tested and measured.

♦ Identify members of the team who are effective at teaching others (not all members are good teachers and coaches). As much as possible, have these people train other members, rather than bringing in outsiders to do the training.

♦ Proceed with training in an orderly and regular fashion. Avoid sessions that run too long or are irregular. Solicit feedback from the team members being trained.

♦ Have members identify the methods of testing for competency. When a team member is ready for testing, have the team oversee the qualification process.

Q&A #1

♦ Encourage the team to develop rewards and recognition for successful job sharing among members. Discourage any reward or reinforcement (including negative reinforcement) for those who oppose job sharing.

Introducing Team Budgeting

Sometimes the introduction of a brand-new task can re-energize the team. One such task that often comes in the middle years is team budgeting.

Budgeting is a rather complex task. It should be transferred to the team in pieces or components until the team is ready to take on the whole process. If the transfer is done too quickly, the team will feel overwhelmed and reject the process altogether. Team members will need to be trained in the specific components of budgeting, including:

♦ Setting organization and departmental priorities
♦ Planning line-item expenses (e.g., salaries, equipment, general expenses)
♦ Using historical data to build an effective budget
♦ Finding resources (comptroller, department head) for information and assistance

As the team maintains its own budget, members will need to be skilled at:

+ Understanding and using the organization's particular budgetary system
+ Breaking an annual budget into monthly amounts and tracking expenses month to month
+ Identifying when a payment has been made and tracking the expense
+ Monitoring expenses to make adjustments in decision making
+ Preparing and delivering reports

Taking responsibility for budgeting or anything related to finances can strongly empower a team, since it is then able to make its own decisions about how much money to spend (within certain predefined boundaries). In addition, members begin to see how their accomplishments affect the whole. These two new insights are very effective motivators for teams in the middle years.

Using Pilot Teams for Team Presentations

The shift to a team culture typically begins with a pilot team or two, which are launched significantly ahead of the rest of the organization. As management makes the decision to move the whole organization toward teams, these pilot teams also need refreshing. One method for achieving this is to allow the pilot teams to give presentations in the training of new teams.

Tips for Team Presentations

+ Allow the team to select the member to make the presentation; do not allow management to pick the team presenter.
+ Define the purpose of the presentation and help the team presenter prepare in advance by reviewing sample questions or giving the presentation to a practice audience. Do not assume that people know how to speak in front of groups.
+ If the presentation is a large or important one, encourage

Q&A
#7

team members to do a "practice presentation" ahead of time for other teams to help with the jitters.

+ Remind presenters to speak from their own experiences on teams, not about what they've heard or read about other teams. Encourage an even presentation by allowing for the good and the bad. Don't suggest that team members sugarcoat their presentations or allow such distortions.
+ Anticipate that the team may use a presentation format to speak to whatever is bothering its members, including criticizing management about the level of its support. Delay responding to such feedback until you have had adequate time to think through a response. Most important, do not respond during any presentation.
+ Use an experienced facilitator to moderate any panel presentations done by teams.
+ Do not allow team members to be attacked by audience members who don't want or like teams. Set clear ground rules in the beginning that allow a facilitator to intervene.
+ Rotate the function of presenter among all members of the team who wish to speak in front of others.
+ Be sure to include any accomplishments in this area in the team's performance review.

At one manufacturing site, eight employees from five different teams participated in a panel discussion held for the benefit of the rest of the organization. Team members responded to all types of questions, and their participation made the whole process more believable for the audience. As the team members talked, they identified their difficulties and their successes. The process of sharing stories and helping to prepare new teams served as a strong refresher for the panelists.

Strategies for Re-Energizing Managers and Supervisors

In an effort to get functional and cross-functional teams up and running, organizations often emphasize training hourly staff. However, it is equally important to provide advance training for managers and supervisors who are responsible for driving the culture change through the organization. Too often a select few managers are trained, and the rest are left out. The pilot teams are launched, and then suddenly the organization finds that it needs managers skilled in team building and there are none. It's better to include all managers early on and train them slowly and steadily over time.

Management and supervisory training needs to focus on the process of empowerment, emphasizing both task completion and the development of relationship skills. Managers especially tend to deny the need for interpersonal relationship skill building. It's important to base the decision whether training is needed in this area on hard data, not on personal opinion. Many feedback tools exist to help training coordinators assess accurately the skills of management and supervisory personnel.

Sample Training Units for Managers and Supervisors

Understanding Empowerment
    The Components Required for Empowerment
    Moving a Workforce Toward Empowerment
    The Core Values and Guiding Principles Required in an
        Empowered Environment
Assessing Workforce Readiness
    Determining Technical Skill Competency
    Determining Behavioral Skill Competency
    Checking Attitude Readiness
    Identifying Driving and Restraining Forces
    Understanding Why Resistance Occurs
Assessing Management Readiness
    Understanding the Cycle of Involvement, Techniques for
        Handling Resistance
    Determining Current Style of Interaction
    Identifying Management Competencies
Developing an Empowerment Plan
    Setting Specific Unit Goals for Empowerment
    Creating an Effective Action Plan for Empowerment
    Gaining Group Agreement and Buy-in
    Who, When, Where, and How to Hand Off

Training Others to Do Your Work
  Determining What Needs to Be Taught and the Best Way
    to Teach It
  Understanding How Adults Learn
  Understanding How Best to Share Information
  Teaching Group Problem Solving and Decision Making
  Defining the Role of Coach
Building Relationships
  Recognizing the Components of Effective Relationships
  Understanding Trust: How It Is Built and Destroyed
  The Best and the Worst Ways to Give and Get Feedback
  Maintaining Meaningful Feedback Scoreboards
Creating a Highly Motivated Environment
  Understanding What Motivates People
  Assessing the Current Environment
  Identifying Intrinsic and Extrinsic Rewards
  Providing Effective Rewards for Empowered and Self-
    directed Teams
Moving from Empowerment to Teams
  Creating Problem-solving and Project Teams
  Creating Self-directed Work Teams

We also recommend four laboratory trainings for managers, supervisors, and professional staff on encouraging interpersonal skill development, improving meeting skills, understanding anger and team conflicts, and developing techniques for resolving team conflicts. Assessment tools administered throughout the training can be very effective at giving immediate feedback and forming baseline data.

Tips for Managerial Training

- Divide the modules into a series of six or eight at a time, and then allow "time-off" periods between module sets. Too much training will reduce retention and use of material.
- Vary the training approach to include role play, case study, panel presentations, simulations, field trips, group discussion, and experiential exercises.

- Expect some resistance to any training techniques that put the manager or supervisor in a vulnerable position. Providing advance knowlede of the exercises that involve risk taking seems to improve participation.
- Always explain the purpose of any activity both before the activity and at the end. Do not assume that managers will intuitively understand why an activity is being done.
- Provide as much celebration and reward for managerial and supervisory personnel as for hourly staff. Do not assume that they don't need hoopla; they do.
- Have managers and supervisors participate in the twenty-five core team training units as well if they have not had team-building training.

The transition for supervisors and managers in the team environment is a difficult one, and the traditional approach of simply providing training is not adequate. Two other strategies—mentoring and journaling—can help supervisors and managers make the transition.

Mentoring

Participants often comment that people act one way in the training room and very differently out with the workforce. To counter this tendency, we launched a mentoring program in conjunction with professional staff training that has been very successful. Each staff member is assigned a mentor (see Chapter 8) who is responsible for:

- Helping the participant apply the training to the worksite
- Encouraging and praising all attempts at new skill development
- Instilling accountability
- Holding weekly meetings to focus on:
  —What did you learn in training?
  —How does what you learned apply to your work setting?
  —Have you identified anything you could experiment with?
  —What have you tried? How did it go?

—Are you having any problems with any of the training?
+ Reviewing the critical-incident journal (described in the following section) with the participant to examine specific incidents and how they were handled
+ Keeping a record of the sessions and the topics of discussion

Tips for Mentors

+ Listen to participant concerns, issues, and ideas.
+ Ask questions (both direct and open-ended).
+ Tell what you've done in a similar situation, but do not tell the employee what to do.
+ Suggest resources to consult when questions come up.
+ Encourage risk taking by offering to role-play situations with the employee until he is able to be successful.
+ Offer gentle feedback (when invited).

Mentoring is not:

+ Telling someone how she should do something
+ Taking over and doing a task for the person
+ Scolding, criticizing, or making sarcastic remarks to get someone to change his behavior
+ Thinking you have to have all the answers
+ Checking up on someone to be certain she is telling the truth or completing assignments
+ Counseling someone by trying to uncover the motives behind the behavior

Sample Format for a Mentoring Session

1. Greet the person, and do some friendly chitchat.
2. Ask some open-ended questions (e.g., What did you think of the training session? Have you had a chance to write in your journal yet?).
3. Ask the person to describe her work area in some detail—the people, the issues, the demands on time—to really get a good sense of what she is dealing with.

4. Ask if he has any new ideas about empowerment for his area. Has he tried anything in particular? How did it go?
5. Speak to your own situation (remember this is a conversation, not a performance review) and some of the ideas you are trying out.
6. Ask if there are particular ways you can be helpful.
7. Close the discussion by confirming the next discussion time.

Journaling

The critical-incident journal provides each training participant with a concrete method of determining the amount of progress being made throughout training. Journaling is a proven technique for improving awareness, understanding, and retention. To use this technique:

1. Obtain from your mentor a notebook to record on-the-job situations that occur throughout the weeks of training.

2. Write down in considerable detail any situation you've tried to improve (and empower), the specific strategies tried, and how they've worked out. You should expect that some strategies will work and others won't. Spelling, punctuation, grammar, and handwriting are irrelevant.

3. As a variation, divide each page in half with a center line. On one half of the page, record your behaviors; on the other half, list at least two options for making the action more effective the next time.

4. Keep the journal confidential. It is wise to use initials or fictitious names to protect people. No one should read the contents of another person's journal without the person's permission.

5. Review the journal notes with your mentor on a regular basis. The idea is not to judge or criticize but to review the situation, discuss the attempted strategy and what worked or didn't, and explore other options. The mentor may encourage role-playing or other strategies to encourage skill development. It's a way to shift discussion from "How are things?" "Oh, fine" to "Let's

review your journal and see what you've been trying out this week."

Managers and supervisors often feel particularly vulnerable in the culture shift to teams. Their jobs are changing dramatically even as they are responsible for changing others. Often they are as confused about where the process is going and what the next steps will be as the teams are. Long-term success of the teams is highly dependent on the level of morale of the management staff.

Maintaining Management and Supervisory Staff Morale

- Identify the benefits of teams for managers and supervisors on a regular basis. Do not assume that they know or see the benefits on their own.
- Openly discuss reservations. Managers and supervisors have lots of fears about the new culture but feel uncomfortable discussing them openly. Create opportunities for discussion.
- Do not try to oversell the new culture. Nothing, including teams, is perfect.
- Acknowledge that some employees like the traditional role of managing or supervising.
- Work as diligently to define new, exciting roles for managers and supervisors as for the teams.
- Give managers and supervisors specific new tasks to do or problems to solve that put them right in the thick of things. Do not let them stay on the fringe too long.
- Mentor those with a poor attitude, and put specific boundaries on their negative behavior. Don't underestimate the power of one bad apple.
- As much as possible, have them identify their own training needs and even participate as cotrainers whenever feasible.

QUESTIONS AND ANSWERS:
Keeping It Fresh

1. **Q.** *As a manager, what can I do when I see a project team continually put off meetings and push back deadlines?*

A. This situation is one of those tricky ones that may look like a conduct issue (resistance or personality differences) but in fact may be more a team competency issue. Perhaps members are not certain how to proceed, what the goal is, or how to run an effective meeting. I'd explore the competency issue first to rule out those possibilities and then investigate the conduct issues. Remember that people often describe problems as relationship issues when in fact many of the relationship issues disappear when competency is improved.

2. **Q.** *On the outside, our team looks like it functions well. However, all we really do is come together as independent members every other week to exchange information. Is there something we could do to make it exciting again?*

    A. Again, I would focus on structural issues. How old is the team's goal? Would revisiting the vision and mission of the team help? Sit down and talk with other members about your thoughts, and ask for theirs. Others may be frustrated as well. The problem may be the way the agenda is formatted. Or it could be that people expected the team to function this way and never considered that it operate differently. How about a field trip to another organization with similar types of teams? I have seen field trips work wonders in getting people juiced up again. Just don't give up until you've explored many different ideas.

3. **Q.** *Why do some teams like games while others don't? People learn better when they're having fun, don't they?*

    A. I find that games are tricky in training. For example, a group of managers and supervisors in an empowerment training series once strongly objected to an activity I asked them to do involving singing. I wanted them to experience what it was like to be leaderless. They broke into small groups—about seven to a group—and were given the words to "My Country 'Tis of Thee" to sing. The object of the exercise was to get them to experience the discomfort of trying to get started and to stay together without a leader. Although they completed the exercise, the whole purpose got lost in the anger they felt about being asked to sing. In fact, by the time the second set of participants came in for training, they were set to refuse to sing. As we talked about their feelings, some interesting insights emerged. They felt that singing is quite a personal activity; because it was the first module of training, they weren't ready to expose themselves yet. They needed the trainers to do something that made themselves vulnerable first, so that it wouldn't seem as if the trainers were enjoying making the participants uncomfortable. They needed a much more extensive description of the purpose of the exercise, repeated after the exercise was over. We were able to use this situation as a worthwhile learning experience, but there were hostile moments in the beginning.

4. **Q.** *Should you give teams responsibility for handling discipline problems as a new task to keep things fresh?*

   A. Team discipline is an area that must be carefully developed. Just as you train managers and supervisors on how to handle discipline because of the legal and personnel issues, so you must train a team. In the early development of the team, it often works best if members try to work with the problem employee for a bit but then hand off the disciplinary action (e.g., first verbal warning, written warning) to management. However, I have seen a very committed new team handle the removal of a team member very well by focusing on the problem behavior rather than on the person, using sound communication and conflict skills (see Chapter 5), documenting all their discussions, seeking advice from the human resources department throughout the process, and taking a strong stand with which it felt comfortable. The member was transferred to an area that still had a traditional structure, had difficulty there as well, and was finally discharged. All the team's documentation was combined with the rest of management's documentation in the employee's file.

5. **Q.** *Our team is ready and willing to participate in any hard-skills training but really balks at the interpersonal-skills training. How can we get members to buy into their need for this type of training?*

A. It really isn't a matter of either/or. The team will need both. I'd suggest two ideas. First, ask the team to complete a team assessment, which will help identify both technical and behavioral issues. Then have members discuss the results as a group and develop a plan for tackling any deficiencies. Usually, training is the preferred remedy. Second, ask the process observers to keep notes on the team's behavior during a month's worth of meetings, and then ask all the process observers to give the team feedback. Usually a group of process observers will give more honest feedback than one individual. I'd also suggest breaking the interpersonal training into minipresentations and asking each member to prepare an overview of one area for the team. For example, a team member could gather materials on listening skills, work up a brief ten- or fifteen-minute presentation, and share the information with the team at the next meeting. If this is done at every meeting, over time the team will acquire new skills.

6. **Q.** *There are a lot of consultants and trainers who say that they are experts at team building. How do you make sure you're hiring the right one?*

A. You're right. I'd ask lots of probing questions about their work with teams and not allow the discussion to focus solely on philosophy or theory. Look for years of experience and depth of experience in any one location. Then I'd get on the phone with organizations listed as references (add a few from the client list who may not be listed as references) and ask them lots of questions about the consultant. You're especially looking for whether the consultant laid out his plan and the company simply followed it or whether the consultant was flexible and skilled enough to let the company create its own plan with guidance from the consultant. The latter leaves the company empowered; the former leaves the company dependent.

7. **Q.** *I like the idea of having team members speak on panels and give presentations, but how can I trust that they will give the right answers when under pressure?*

A. I'm always pleasantly surprised at how competent, composed, and prepared team members are when they sit on panels or give presentations. Remember, they're in the spotlight and want to look and act their best. If you still have doubts, do a practice session with them and see how they do.

8. **Q.** *The research on job sharing suggests that organizations need to do certain things to encourage teams to share jobs more readily. What ideas do you have?*

A. Organizations need to address a number of issues, particularly the impact of age and status on job sharing. The organization needs to try to find a path for those who are willing to switch or share jobs. For example, if only one employee can operate a piece of equipment and he won't participate in job switching, then that path is blocked for any employee who does wish to learn new skills. Organizations are also going to have to deal with the impact of age on job-switching behavior. They will have to consider minimizing status differences by providing minimum-level job switching and avoiding assigning workers to primary job classifications.

Note

1. Marvin Blumberg, "Job Switching in Autonomous Work Groups," in *Classic Readings in Self-Managing Teamwork*, ed. Rollin Glaser (King of Prussia, Pa.: Organization Design and Development, 1992), pp. 194–221.

4
Building Strategic Relationships

Relationships are defined as the connections between and among people. Dr. Margaret Wheatley in her book *Leadership and the New Science* has stated, "We don't know who we are until we are in relationship with a person, event or something else."[1] Nothing is as essential to effective teams as team members' ability to relate to one another. In a society where divorce is the common remedy for relationship difficulty, team members struggle with why they have to work harder on their relationships at work than they do at home. In the past, the supervisor separated people who were intolerant of each other; management dictated the consequences of not getting along; someone always intervened to keep sour relationships in check. As one team member said, "When someone bugged me in the past, I'd go drive the forklift and ignore him."

Now team members must be able to work together, as well as with management, customers, supervisors, suppliers, and members of other teams within and outside the organization. Teams have to know how to handle people who don't want to be on teams, build interteam alliances, resolve petty squabbles and heated arguments, share technical staff—even benchmark with teams from other companies. The relationship demands are endless. For people with little experience building and maintaining relationships, the learning curve is very steep and the stress is enormous.

Common Stressors for Teams

- Learning all the technical and behavioral skills necessary to function well as a team while the team is functioning on a day-to-day basis
- Getting all team members to accept responsibility and accountability
- Shifting the role of supervisor to that of facilitator/coach
- Allocating time between team activities and regular work
- Providing clear and meaningful authority for the team
- Resolving conflicts with established policies, procedures, systems, structures, and people
- Overcoming early mistakes and exaggerations

These stressors get acted out in the relationships on the team and can bond or divide the team, depending on the level of relationship skill that members are able to demonstrate.

A resource team of six engineers in a utility company spent hours talking about morale problems and getting nowhere. As we analyzed the patterns in their communication, it became clear that each person would speak to his point of view but rarely respond to the person who had spoken before him. Each person would do the same, going deeper and deeper into the topic but never acknowledging what had already been said; speakers neglected to link speakers' comments or even decide as a group how intensely they wanted to discuss the issue. To their pattern of relating, they had to identify the components in effective relationships and specific behaviors that they needed and were willing to change.

Elements in an Effective Relationship

Relationships don't just happen; they require work. These basic principles must be shared by all the people in the team relationship:

- The belief that the other people are trustworthy, will do you no harm, and, in fact, have the team's best interests in mind.

- An agreement that each member will tell the truth as he or she knows it.
- An ability and a willingness to communicate about all types of issues, including those that might result in a difference of opinion.
- Recognition of other people's attributes, interests, and achievements. Liking a team member is not as important as recognizing that the member has something to contribute to the team.
- Clarity about how decisions will be made and by whom.
- Self-respect that allows team members to establish appropriate boundaries in their relationships so that members can be separate people with their own opinions, ideas, and mindsets.
- A desire to share time, space, concepts, workload, and frustrations with team members.
- Self-awareness, as demonstrated by a willingness to delay judgment and examine and change specific personal behaviors that hamper team success.

A third-shift maintenance employee had been with the company for more than eighteen years. When the area became a self-directed team, he told us that he had no idea how to relate to other people. As a child he had done poorly in school, had few friends, and considered himself a loner. In fact, he liked the night shift because it meant he didn't have to talk to anyone. His self-esteem was very low. He would often say, "Why do they want to know what I think?" Breaking out of this cycle of thinking is not easy, but with consistent, long-term coaching and encouragement, people can change. In the maintenance worker's case, the organization provided mentoring support (see Chapter 3) and assisted him with additional schooling and counseling. Today he facilitates team meetings, functions as a team leader, sits on a cross-functional production team, and is a strong supporter of teams.

That's not to suggest that all relationships work out perfectly. Most teams experience ongoing relationship difficulties throughout their history; some problems remain low-grade annoyances, while others fester constantly.

Typical Relationship Difficulties on Teams

+ Personality and style differences that make it difficult for one person to tolerate another person's behavior
+ Members' use of a condescending manner when referring to people and their work on teams
+ Attacks that challenge teams, team members, and other personnel
+ Poor handling of conflicts between members
+ Old broken promises or disappointments that still influence team members' behaviors
+ Failure of team members to admit when they are wrong, have lost something, or have forgotten to do something affecting the team and to offer an apology
+ Inconsistent actions or thoughtless remarks from those overseeing the team's development
+ Competition among members with similar needs
+ Issues related to the shifting of power and control
+ Cover-ups or displays of arrogance arising out of lack of skill or competency
+ Differences of opinions that become exaggerated and divisive

Teams don't like to admit that problems exist. There are still some people who believe that people on teams don't disagree, argue, bicker, and nag. Consequently, most teams say publicly that they have good relationships but tell a very different story privately. Even though relationship difficulties may not be out in the open, there are usually signs of trouble.

Signs of Relationship Problems

+ Glib or cutting humor, particularly at the expense of another team member
+ Uncomfortable silence that suggests a power struggle (e.g., "Go ahead and try to make me participate")
+ Agendas that focus on information sharing to avoid real discussion and problem solving
+ Body language (e.g., suggesting a closed mind and with-

drawal from the group members who sit with arms folded
or at some distance from other members)
+ Informal meetings of a few team members after the regular
team meeting ends
+ Lots of nonverbal communication (eye rolling, arm folding)
between members
+ Under-the-table remarks and jabs at various team members
+ Seating patterns that allow the same people always to sit
next to each other or that allow some people to sit around
the table and force others to be seated at a distance

The administrative team at a small college had a difficult time
with the head of the organization, who always took over the team
meetings. The president would berate members, criticize their
work in front of other team members, and dictate how decisions
would be made. After each meeting, the team would secretly
meet for another thirty minutes without him, just to soothe in-
jured members and work on strategies for dealing with a difficult boss.

Strengthening Relationships on a Team

Improving team relationships requires a commitment by every
member to work on a set of new skills, including listening, asking
good questions, providing helpful feedback, recognizing the difference between acceptance and agreement, and confronting
when necessary in an affective manner. Members also need to
recognize that different members see things differently.

Improving the Team's Listening Skills

Most people believe they are good listeners, so often the first step
in improving listening skills is to get team members to recognize
that they are "learners in listening." By comparing the amount of
formal study allotted for learning how to read and write in school
with the amount of formal study in listening and speaking, people begin to see the gap, especially when it's put in terms of the

amount of time they spend on the job reading and writing and speaking and listening.

Listening requires tremendous self-discipline to keep the mind from wandering or beginning its own rebuttal. As an experiment, read a brief newspaper story to one team member and ask the person to repeat it to another team member, and so on down the line. By the time the story gets to the last person, it's guaranteed to be a different story.

A resource team of managers for a construction company objected to the idea of paraphrasing each other's comments during a team discussion in order to practice listening skills. One member stated emphatically, "I am very skilled at listening and see no value in restating what another member of the team has said. We don't have time for that!" Thirty minutes later he was caught not having listened to instructions given by another team member for how to complete a specific form. Still he emphasized his ability to listen and blamed the speaker for not being clear.

Requirements for Effective Listening

- Hearing what is said so carefully that the team member can restate and paraphrase precisely the speaker's comment
- Identifying what the person feels strongly about and why the person feels strongly about it
- Exercising self-discipline over one's own behaviors (e.g., doodling, interrupting, fiddling)
- Asking questions that encourage a person to expand upon what he/she is saying
- Learning to pause for response when asking questions or making comments about what has been said
- Referring back to points made earlier by the speaker and building on those ideas
- Offering suggestions and explaining one's own feelings
- Controlling body language that does not convey interest and involvement in what the other person is saying

Barriers to Effective Listening

- Poorly organized presentation by the speaker
- Poor word choices and inappropriate or distracting nonverbal communication by the speaker

* Speaker's failure to state early on why the message may be of interest or value
* Inaccurate information from the speaker
* Speakers use of emotional trigger words that distract the listener
* Listener's concentration on rebuttal
* Listener's reactions to speaker's clothing, manner, mood
* Listener's impatience and interruption
* A disruptive setting
* Listener's focus on her own needs as she pretends to listen to the speaker

During a training session we asked each member to write what he or she felt about a current event on a piece of paper. Then one member expressed his point of view and the next person in the circle had to paraphrase it. When the paraphrase was completed accurately the listener became the speaker and moved on around the circle. Three observations emerged: listeners often had difficulty paraphrasing accurately and added to or embellished what the person had said on the basis of what the listener wanted to be saying; listeners allowed speakers to go on and on without checking for clarity or writing down the speaker's points; and speakers often accepted the erroneous paraphrase in order to avoid saying, "No, you didn't hear me correctly."

More issues are involved in listening than we may realize: Are we willing to give up control to another person? Are we ready to acknowledge the worth of another's ideas? Are we keeping score of who has had the most "floor time"? Real listening requires subordinating the self for the benefit of the team, giving up individual power and control to gain power and control as a team.

Types of Listening

There are two main types of listening: reflective and interpretive.

Reflective listening includes *restating* and *paraphrasing*. Restating (repeating back to the person exactly what she has said) is particularly effective when you want the person to rethink and reevaluate what she has said: Team Member: "We ought to forget all about teams and bring back supervisors!" Response: "We

Q&A
#2

ought to forget all about teams and bring back supervisors.") Often the person will then say, "Well, maybe not all the supervisors." Restating works as long as you don't raise your voice at the end as if you are asking a question.

Paraphrasing or rephrasing reiterates the speaker's statement in different words. Stephen Covey in his best-selling book *Seven Habits of Highly Effective People*[2] stresses the importance of the rule "Seek first to understand before seeking to be understood." We all have a tendency to immediately respond to another person's statement or question rather than spending a few minutes trying to understand what the person is expressing and why. To paraphrase effectively:

- Begin by listening for the feelings behind the words and then lead with: "It sounds like . . ."; "I get the sense . . ."; "If I understand correctly . . ."; "In other words . . ."
- Use a tentative tone of voice to indicate that you are asking whether your interpretation is correct.
- Avoid using words that could upset someone (e.g., "It sounds like you're bitter about Jill's getting the job").

Both restating and paraphrasing require lots of practice. Don't allow team members off the hook when they respond, "Oh, I know how to do that." Require role-play demonstration before the entire team.

Interpretative listening, the second kind of listening, requires the listener to try to identify the hidden messages or hidden feelings behind what is being said (e.g., "It sounds like you're feeling overwhelmed with all your team responsibilities").

To listen interpretively:

- Listen with your ears and your eyes. Pay attention to vocal tone, inflection, body posture, and gestures in order to uncover what the person is feeling.
- Give full attention to what the other person is saying. Do not focus on what you plan to say next.
- Put the other person's feelings or messages into words.
- Help clarify feelings by giving insight and perspective to a situation.

+ Demonstrate that having feelings and talking about feelings is okay.
+ Avoid labeling negative feelings in the extreme (use frustrated for angry; disappointed for sad or upset).

Tips for Improving Team Members' Listening Skills

+ Periodically require the team to go through exercises in restating, paraphrasing, and interpreting to improve or sharpen their listening skills.
+ Encourage members to jot down the speaker's key points on a piece of paper so that they can refer back to them later. Have a member record key thoughts during discussion on a flipchart so that members can rephrase often.
+ Practice intense listening, such as that required when trying to identify musical instruments in an orchestra.
+ Assign a team member the responsibility of keeping track of the key points made in a discussion and summarizing them periodically for the team throughout the meeting. While this is often the facilitator's job, asking another member to do it for the team can improve listening.
+ Encourage the process observers to assess the team's listening capability (where did we listen to each other well? where did we make mistakes because we didn't listen to each other?) during their periodic feedback sessions with the team. Of course, process observers can intervene during a meeting as well if they feel that members are not listening to each other.
+ Suggest that members give individual feedback to other members who have a tendency not to listen (e.g., "At yesterday's meeting, I felt you didn't really hear the point I was trying to make").
+ Explore with members what they are doing when they are not listening (e.g., framing their own rebuttal, daydreaming, remembering the need to do a particular task).
+ Do not allow team members to raise their hands when another team member is speaking. A team member who shoots her hand up in the middle of someone's sentence signals to the speaker that something he or she has said is

wrong (whether it is or not) and the speaker typically will begin diluting his or her point.

Empathetic Listening

We can also be listening for what is being said when nothing is actually said. Empathy comes from the Greek for "feel in"; it means the ability to feel what another person is feeling. Listening increases empathy as we try to understand and affirm another's feelings.

Listening will improve only when members accept and agree that it is important for them to do so. It's not enough that one or two team members are good listeners and as a result overfunction for team members who are not. The entire team must be expert listeners, not only for their team relationships but for their relationships with people outside the team.

Not only do team members have to become adept at listening to each other; with the advent of teams, they must be able to listen well to other teams, especially those outside their work unit.

Listening Outside the Team

- Listen carefully to the details of a problem concerning another team, group or individual.
- Listen for both facts and feelings.
- Ask many questions to gather as much information as possible.
- Try to identify the need expressed by the other team as well as the goal the other team, group, or individual wants to achieve.
- Link your goal to the other team's goal. Listen for points that you can both agree on.
- Recognize and accept that people outside the team may not have had interpersonal skills training. Members cannot expect nonmembers to give effective feedback, listen well, and seek to understand if they have never learned these skills.
- Increase your level of tolerance and helpfulness in the communication process. Make an extra effort to assist actively in the listening process.

Many teams complain that other people, including managers and supervisors, are not as good at listening as they ought to be. They often enjoy pointing out the errors in other people's presentation ("For a manager, he should have known better than to use 'you' statements on me. Even I know better than that!"). Even when the team member is right, he needs to display patience and tolerance toward the manager until the manager is fully trained as well.

Most team members listen and respond, listen and respond. Relationships are strengthened, however, when we listen (reflectively and interpretively), ask good questions, and then respond. Asking questions, like listening, requires greater skill than we realize.

Learning to Ask Good Questions

Nothing is more effective for building relationships than the ability to ask questions rather than make statements. Statements cause people to position either for or against; questions are like fresh air—they demonstrate how much we value another person and desire to understand her thinking. Good questions have the following characteristics:

+ They begin with the words *who, what, where, when* and *how*.
+ They cannot be answered with a simple yes or no.
+ They help the team focus on issues and evaluate the situation.
+ They encourage team members to say what they think and feel about a situation.
+ They help team members explore a situation from a variety of perspectives.
+ They make the other person feel the team member is paying attention and wants to know more.

There are also questions that it is wise to avoid:

+ Questions that require a yes or no answer and do not help to gather information or continue conversation

- *Why* questions, because they presuppose a specific answer and put people on the defensive by sounding judgmental
- Rapid-fire questions that make a person feel overwhelmed
- Questions that contain the answer ("You're not going to ask him on the team, are you?")
- Questions that begin with *can* and *could* instead of *will* or *would* when someone is being asked to contribute

John Gray, the author of *Men Are From Mars; Women Are From Venus,*[3] has done considerable research on how men respond to the question "Can or could you do this for me?" He suggests that it triggers a subconscious negative response—"Sure I could do it for you, but I'm not saying I will" and recommends using *will* or *would* instead as the question opener.

When eight or ten people get together to form a team, they bring different points of view, past experiences, values and perceptions, and personalities (see Chapter 5 for more information on conflict). For a time, members are nice and polite and put more emphasis on finding similarities than on highlighting differences. This stage is called the Forming Stage.[4] By the time the team enters what is called the Storming Stage, nice is no longer the operative word. As members struggle for power and control ("Who is in charge here, anyway?"), the tolerance for individual differences disappears. The third stage in team development, Norming, is the time that the team develops its procedures; norming requires strengthening the ability to accept member differences and use them to the team's advantage. When a team is able to accomplish this, it has achieved the fourth stage of team development, called Performing.

Acceptance vs. Agreement

A team that is able to accept team member differences is typically capable of distinguishing between acceptance and agreement—a subtle, yet vitally important test of relationship maturity. Acceptance does not mean agreement, or approving another's ideas or behavior. Acceptance is simply acknowledging the worth of another person on the team and keeping an open mind about other's experiences and opinions.

One activity that can help the team explore the issue of acceptance is identifying what helps members accept people who are different from them. Typical responses include the idea of realizing I can be wrong sometimes, walking in their shoes, listening without judging. Then have members identify three things that they are currently dead set against by completing the sentence "I don't agree with people who believe _____, but I still accept that these people have a right to their point of view." Explore as a team how people felt making the statement and whether they really believe it.

Team members demonstrate lack of acceptance of others by:

+ Positioning people immediately as right or wrong
+ Showing intolerance for other viewpoints
+ Criticizing harshly the "wrongness" of others' perspectives
+ Keeping track of past errors and bringing them up at strategic moments
+ Making sarcastic comments, subtle jokes, and cutting remarks

Key Aspects of Acceptance

+ Recognition that people who disagree with us help us to gain a more complete perspective on an issue. Make this point by using the F's exercise (Find the number of F's in the following statement: "Feature films are the results of years of scientific study combined with many years of experience."). Many people can find only three until those who find six help them out.

+ All of us are incomplete in our knowledge of any topic. When we recognize this fact, it typically brings humility, which is the forerunner of tolerance.

+ It is not necessary to agree with everything someone says in order to be open to accepting part of what he says. If we can see the whole as a collection of parts and isolate the parts we can accept, we can begin to find common ground.

+ Acceptance makes us feel vulnerable because we hold a misconception that disagreeing is powerful and agreeing diminishes power. Effective teams recognize that the reverse is true.

The Value of Vulnerability

The desire to have better relationships begins with a softening of the heart—a willingness to be vulnerable, to say "I don't know" instead of "I know" all the time—exactly the opposite of what American business has encouraged in the past. The following checklist helps teams determine whether the foundation for relationship building is strong or weak.

Do team members:

+ Withdraw from relationships that require them to get close?
+ Tend to avoid getting involved in other people's lives?
+ Act suspicious of people who are too friendly?
+ Seem friendly only with people they've known for a long time?
+ Rarely open up with people?
+ Seem uncomfortable displaying appropriate affection toward other members?
+ Usually cover up any expression of real emotion?
+ Seem uncomfortable around people who openly express their emotions?
+ Have to appear to be right all the time?
+ Exaggerate their role or importance in any given situation?

This process of sharing the self and accepting different viewpoints is important for the team to explore in depth. Members need to get comfortable sitting and listening to each other without needing to "fix" each other. The repeated act of going around the table and hearing members express their feelings without judgment or remedy will increase the willingness of members to be vulnerable. While it is tempting to try to fix the problem and remove the pain, real growth comes when team members recognize that their only role is to accept, understand, and support each other.

Key Behaviors for Encouraging Acceptance and Vulnerability

+ Ask open-ended questions (e.g., How do you feel about this? What examples come to mind?)

- Share personal experiences that include the expression of facts and feelings.
- Acknowledge mistakes quickly. The elements of a sincere apology include: offer it soon, be specific about your behavior, be sincere in the offer, express regret, make restitution, and take responsibility for your error.
- Take moments to connect with appropriate, careful touching that expresses acceptance and support. Reaching out helps people know they are accepted.
- Spend time together talking, listening, sharing, interacting.
- Avoid judging and evaluating each other.
- Avoid thinking of people in terms of us and them.
- Cultivate the habit of speaking well of others by seeing good qualities rather than errors and failings.

Gentle Confrontation

Part of being in an effective relationship is the understanding that there will be times when team members must gently confront each other about behaviors, actions, and assumptions that are causing problems in relationships. Sometimes team members have to ask a member to stop and reconsider his words and actions; sometimes members need to be corrected about their descriptions of what really happened in a situation. Confrontation provides a team member with information about himself, encourages the team member to take responsibility for his actions and words, and motivates the member to change behavior. The person doing the confronting must have courage and a belief that the relationship will be strengthened in the end.

Characteristics of Gentle Confrontation

- Use a format such as "You say or you feel _____, but the truth is _____." Another format is "I feel (state feeling) when you (state behavior) because (state reason.)"[5]
- Confrontation must be motivated by true caring for the team member. When it is motivated by anger, revenge, or

Q&A
#9

insecurity, the team member feels criticized, condemned, and rejected.

+ The goal must be to benefit the team member.
+ Confrontation should be used only when trust has already been established on the team.
+ Confrontation must focus on specific behaviors or contradictions that can be corrected.

Use gentle confrontation when:

+ A discrepancy exists between two statements that a person makes
+ A contradiction exists between what the team member is saying and how the team member is acting
+ A team member is rationalizing or excusing her behavior
+ A team member uses false assumptions or misinformation (e.g., "Well, nobody can really reach consensus, anyway")
+ A discrepancy exists between what the team member says he or she said and what other team members witnessed

Sometimes even with the best listening and sharing, people have difficulty building relationships. Personality differences polarize team members before they even get close to problem solving. The ability to see these differences in style and approach and use them to add value is critical to strengthening the team's work.

Understanding Personalities

In the mid-1920s, the Swiss psychoanalyst Carl Jung explored in his book *Psychological Types* the idea that every person develops primacy in one of our major behavioral functions: intuiting, thinking, feeling, and sensing.[6] He claimed that behavioral patterns are determined genetically and that, despite using a blend of styles, each person relies heavily on a dominant style. By recognizing the characteristics of each style, team members are better able to appreciate the differences and use them to the team's advantage.

The Four Functional Styles

The *intuitors* live in the world of ideas, inventions, and global concepts, often questioning why things are done a certain way. They enjoy delving into problem solving with a single-minded focus and creating multiple strategies at the drop of a hat. Intuitors like to challenge authority and quickly reject ideas that are based on the boss's saying so. Typically, they are not strong in completing details and follow-through. They have little regard for time and often annoy other team members because they give priority to their plans and projects. They can be sarcastic if others do not quickly grasp the significance of their idea.

The *thinkers* see the world from the neck up—information, facts, data, logic, systems. Thinker team members have an orderly manner and desire structure and control; they like budgets, procedures, and policies. Success for the thinker is being correct; perfectionism and procrastination are two characteristic traits. Their speech and their decisions are usually slow and deliberate, as they like to take time to reflect, analyze, review, and revise.

The *feelers* view the world from the neck down, stressing relationships and harmony on the team. Their involvement on the team is based on past experiences more than on future possibilities or facts. They like the social niceties associated with teams, often feeling slighted if the team gets right down to business too fast. The feelers are the first to accommodate the other styles.

The *sensor* wants results. Sensors take responsibility for the action items in the team meeting and like to make things happen. They create competition even if it means defeating neighboring teams. They take control of conversations, usually getting right to the point and expecting others to do the same. Sensors are always on the move, use to-do lists, and have little patience with slow-moving types. Verbal sparring is an often misunderstood characteristic trait; sensors spar only with people they like and respect.

It quickly becomes obvious who's who on teams. It's important when doing style work with the teams to stress that everyone has all four styles in him or her and that no single style is preferred above any other. A discussion of styles is also an excellent opportunity to demonstrate that teams can get into conflicts more over a style than substance. For example, a team of all four styles may decide to give a summary report of its work at a company meeting. Most likely, the intuitor has given her ideas early on but hasn't helped at all with pulling the data together. The sensor is bossing everyone around, which is making the feeler very anxious. The thinker believes that the team needs to wait for just another piece or two of data before photocopying the report. The delay tactic has the sensor ballistic, which prompts the feeler to cry out, "Why can't we just all try to get along?"

Learning to Flex Styles

Most people have been fishing at some time in their lives. Flexing styles is much like baiting the hook when you're fishing. When communicating, most people bait the hook to suit themselves (e.g., "Look, this is the way I am; I'm too old to change"). Effective teams must learn how to flex to the styles of other members in order to improve communication and capitalize on the strengths of each style brings to the team. This includes teaching team members with each of the four styles the specific behaviors they can exhibit that will help others with other styles to relax and communicate more openly:

1. *Flexing for the intuitor.* Hook the intuitors by asking a question or seeking help with a problem. Do not come with the problem solved; they have no interest in a finished product. Enjoy rambling with intuitors a bit (we call it kite flying), bringing them back to the issue every once in a while in a gentle manner. Use words like *idea, cyberspace,* and *cutting edge.* Accommodate their inability to perform detail work.

2. *Flexing for the thinker.* Set up a time to meet in advance. Do your homework, come prepared, and check for little mistakes that will make the thinker disbelieve the entire idea. Talk slowly and deliberately, using calm hand gestures, and remain self-contained. Discuss plans and ask for relevant history. Expect to have to set up a second or third meeting if a decision is required.

3. *Flexing for the feeler.* Spend time in the beginning chatting about recent events other than work. Use *we* and *together* and express the need to have this person on the team. Share stories

about people to illustrate your point. Do not rush the feelers into decisions; anticipate that they will have to check with others to see what the general consensus is before committing to a specific action.

4. *Flexing for the sensor.* Do not set up an appointment. Drop by and say, "Do you have a minute?" Use crisp, direct, action or sports-based words. Speak of the results that can be achieved, not the process for getting there. Anticipate some verbal sparring; prepare to give some back. Act confident and assertive.

The next step is for the team to learn to appreciate the value of each style for the team. One secretarial team, for example, realized that it had no strong intuitors. As a result, it made a conscious decision to require brainstorming in all its problem solving. It recognized that it would be tempting—yet in error—to bypass brainstorming and go directly to implementing the first idea presented.

The Myers-Briggs Type Indicator (MBTI), published by Consulting Psychologists Press, is another widely used instrument for establishing individual personality preferences and encouraging the constructive use of differences between people. The MBTI tool can help team members recognize how their personality types influence decision making, as well as assist a team during member selection in being certain to have the full range of personality choices on the team.[7]

When a team is formed, people are often under the mistaken assumption that everything will be fine if the focus is on getting the task done. They fail to recognize the impact of group behavior on the process. Not all group dynamics are positive, as most of us know. It's important for teams to recognize behaviors that can cause serious problems.

Understanding Group Behavior

People are a mixture of two disparate needs: the drive to be individuals and the intense desire to be part of a community. This paradox dramatically affects group dynamics. In 1971 Irving Janis[8] defined eight symptoms of group thought processes that influence a group's ability to make effective decisions. Some of the concepts that he and others have identified are:

- *The Abilene Paradox.*[9] Unvoiced disagreement is the most common problem in organizations. Because people do not speak up about their feelings and thoughts, teams sometimes decide to do things that no one really wants to do.
- *Groupthink.* Individual members of a team sometimes succumb to team pressure even in direct contradiction to their values and goals. People on teams tend to strive for agreement.
- *Group tyranny.* Members sometimes blame a group for their own behavior when it fails to live up to their own standards and values.
- *Illusion of invulnerability.* Believing that the team is immune from error, the team may take extreme risks.
- *Illusion of inherent morality.* Sometimes members develop an unquestioning faith in the group's own morality; they believe that whatever the group decides must be the right ethical or moral choice.
- *Collective rationalization.* The group may come to believe that past success guarantees future success.
- *Direct pressure.* The team may exert pressure on members who do not conform or who express doubts in or question the validity of any of the group's beliefs.
- *Negative stereotyping.* Groups tend to stereotype outsiders negatively, creating an "us versus them" perspective.
- *Pressure for self-censorship.* Members may be willing to devalue their own ideas if they conflict with those of other team members.
- *Mindguarding.* Members sometimes try to protect the team from exposure to ideas that threaten group assumptions.
- *Illusion of unanimity.* Team members may tend to discount any threat to group agreement and to misinterpret silence as indicating agreement with what is being expressed.

Tips on Counteracting Threats to Team Success

- Create and maintain an open, candid climate.
- Avoid insulation. Encourage the team to visit other teams, inside and outside the organization.

Q&A #8

- Avoid being too directive or exerting undue influence.
- Suggest that the team identify a member whose job is to evaluate whether the team is being threatened by counter-productive behaviors.
- Use process observers to provide feedback to the team during meetings.
- Read through this chapter as a team and talk about what the team can do to strengthen its relationships.

QUESTIONS AND ANSWERS:
Building Strategic Relationships

1. **Q.** *How do I convince the team manager that you can't build relationships by E-mail?*

   A. I would encourage you to give the manager feedback (gentle confrontation) about his behavior. It may be necessary for several team members to say the same thing. Be sure to include behaviors that you would like to see.

2. **Q.** *What should you do when a team doesn't accept a new member?*

   A. Often, in the second and third stages of team development, teams don't like to bring in new members unless they have specifically asked for a new person to be added. Here's another good time to use reflective listening, interpretive listening, questions, and gentle confrontation. These help the team to realize how closed it is being.

3. **Q.** *How do you help a team member save face with other team members?*

   A. Teams need to learn how to give "grace" to their members on occasion, giving someone something she has not earned. It may be a special assignment, a pat on the back, an unsolicited hello, or a decision to let a member save face by not having to answer for certain actions. My experience suggests that "grace" needs to be taught as a positive, because many people see it as being weak.

4. **Q.** *How much should you share about one team member with another team or a manager?*

    A. I made the mistake once of sharing with one team the comments of another team without its approval. The oversight team had wanted to know how a secretarial team was progressing. I shared my thoughts and then gave a specific example. It was a big mistake. Always check before sharing information about one team with another.

5. **Q.** *How do you handle someone who likes the powerful feeling of withholding information that other team members need?*

    A. It's best for the team to deal with the person directly. By using the good questions and gentle confrontation model, the team might get the person to release some information. However, information is power, and the underlying issue will have to be dealt with at some point.

6. **Q.** *How do you handle a person who thrives on creating and spreading rumors about team members and other employees?*

    A. Two things need to occur. The team needs to address the person directly about her behavior, and it needs to agree to a person that it will not participate in any gossip and will, in fact, walk away from the person whenever it happens.

7. **Q.** *How do you handle a team member who has a "can't do" attitude and gripes and complains about every new project?*

    A. It's best to explore what actions the member really wants to take and what's keeping the person from doing so. Thinking through the "worse-case scenario" can help to identify realistic and unrealistic fears. Also ask what will happen if the person takes no action, as well as explore how others think and what kind of support they might give the person.

8. **Q.** *Is there an effective strategy to combat groupthink and group tyranny?*

A. There are two good videos, called *Abilene Paradox* and *Group Tyranny*,[10] from CRM films that are helpful discussion openers on the topics of groupthink and group tyranny. Both videos explore the tendency in our nature to "go along with the crowd" even when we don't really agree. After team members have viewed the videos, encourage them to discuss, "Have we ever gone to Abilene?" "When does it happen?" "Do we ever use group tyranny to get our own way?" and "How can we, as a team, combat these tendencies?"

9. **Q.** *How do we get managers to walk the talk, especially when it comes to listening?*

A. This is a much tougher question than we think. Just recently a boss turned to a department manager, pointed his finger right in his face, and said, "You're dead wrong about what's going to happen with this organization in the future. Absolutely dead wrong." In most traditional environments that power play would have gone unchecked. However, in this team environment the process observer raised the help/hinder sheet, saying, "As process observer I need to remind you that we've all agreed not to speak to each other that way." While the boss probably wasn't too happy about the feedback, he did phrase his comments more carefully for the rest of the meeting.

10. **Q.** *You bring up many examples of the team members who are unwilling to focus on relationship issues, but I have the opposite problem. What do you do if you have two team members who are fixated on uncovering all the feelings and "stamps" behind every member's comments?*

A. As we noted in the personality style section of this chapter, some people are more in touch with their feelings than are others. It might be helpful to do some communication styles or Myers-Briggs training and have each member discuss how he or she interacts with the team. It's natural for a team full of "feeler"-style people to focus on relationship issues and for one full of sensors or thinkers to focus on task issues.

Notes

1. Margaret Wheatley, *Leadership and the New Science* (San Francisco: Berrett-Koehler, 1994).
2. Stephen Covey, *Seven Habits of Highly Effective People* (New York: Simon and Schuster, 1989).
3. John Gray, *Men Are From Mars; Women Are From Venus* (HarperCollins, 1992).
4. B. W. Tuckman, "Development Sequence in Small Groups," *Psychological Bulletin* 63 (1965): 384–399.
5. Harriet R. T. Lewis, *Crisis Pregnancy Center Volunteer Training Manual* (Falls Church, Va.: Christian Action Council, 1992), pp. 36–37.
6. John Bledsoe, "Your Four Communicating Styles," *Training, The Magazine of Human Resources Development* (March, 1976).
7. Otto Kroeger, *Type Talk at Work* (New York: Delacorte Press, 1992).
8. I. Janis, "Groupthink," *Psychology Today* (November 1971): 43–46, 74–76.
9. Jerry B. Harvey, *The Abilene Paradox and Other Meditations on Management* (Lexington, Mass.: Lexington Books, 1988).
10. Jerry Harvey, *Group Tyranny and the Gunsmoke Phenomenon* (Carlsbad, Calif.: CRM Films, 1991).

5

Building Trust and Resolving Conflicts

Most teams agree that the process of building and maintaining relationships among team members is their most difficult problem. Bickering, backbiting and gossiping constantly fuel tensions; old "stamps" erupt at the oddest times—and no one is there to referee. The relationship veneer maintained in the old structure disappears in the team environment. Intense daily contact on tasks and the constant thrashing out of differences of opinion place new demands on old relationships. Walking away and ignoring each other are no longer acceptable options. Team members must know how to build trust and simultaneously resolve conflicts in order to survive.

"Stamp Collecting"

Many of us can recall when mom went to the grocery store and at the checkout got a certain number of blue or green stamps; the number was based on the amount of her purchase. She licked the stamps and put them in a book that later could be redeemed for merchandise at a blue- or green-stamp store. Some people on teams collect "stamps" as well, except that these stamps are licked and put in a book when another teammate does something "wrong." Rather than risk discussing the action in the open, a member simply licks a stamp and puts it in his or her memory book. Some people have enough stamps on people to furnish an entire house if the stamps could be converted into merchandise. We call this "stamp collecting."

Some months ago a team member abruptly stopped discussion when he pointed his finger at a supervisor who was helping the team and said, "I remember when I called you for help and you didn't come." The supervisor looked blank and said, "I don't remember when that happened." The team member responded, "When we blew a fuse. You came the first time but not the second time. "The supervisor asked, "Was that this year?" "Nope," the team member responded. Another team member asked, "Well, was it in the nineties?" "Nope," the team member said. "It was in 1987." He had held that stamp for nearly a decade!

Members of the self-directed work team in a cosmetic company found it helpful to say to each other, "I don't want to collect a stamp on this, so can we talk about it?" It became a way to surface what might appear to be an insignificant issue for discussion among the team members.

Typical Team Maintenance Issues

+ Insufficient commitment to the team
+ Reluctance of members to spend energy on team's purpose and goal
+ Tolerance of mediocre participation and contribution
+ A closed climate that prevents members from expressing honestly how they feel about issues.
+ Conflicting personal agendas among team members, resulting in general distrust
+ Impact of unqualified members
+ Lack of effort in developing skills of new members
+ Formation of cliques within the team
+ Lack of shared leadership; inappropriate leadership
+ Poor work methods, resulting in difficulty handling the workload and delay in resolving important issues
+ Lack of role clarity, communication, and administrative procedures
+ Lack of creativity as members conform to the team's standard of operating
+ Lack of ability to work through differences of opinions among members

 • Unwillingness to accept new ideas from outside the team
 • Unwillingness to adapt to changing needs

Sometimes these issues compound to the point where it hardly seems worth the effort to maintain the team. It is important to remember that these same problems exist in traditional organizations as well—it's just that nobody talks openly about them. Although teams may recognize the importance of unity and respect, obstacles often prevent them from achieving a higher level of team interaction.

Bringing New People on Board

The introduction of a new person on the team typically causes the team to take some backward steps. However, there are some strategies to make the transition a smooth one:

 • As much as possible, involve the team in the selection of the new member (see Chapter 8).
 • Ask the team if someone will volunteer to be the new member's "buddy" for a month or so. The buddy is responsible for orienting the new member.
 • Provide the new member with all relevant background information and training material.
 • If the new member lacks training, have the in-house training team (see Chapter 8) do quick, short training sessions to address immediate needs.
 • Anticipate that power and control issues will come up again, especially if the new member is outspoken.

Two self-directed work teams—one in shipping and one in maintenance—spent months giving each other a hard time. They picked on each other mercilessly to the point that tempers flared on a regular basis. Despite numerous attempts to work on building joint goals, it finally came down to having the plant manager say that the behavior must stop. He functioned as an "agreement manager"—drawing the line in the sand—to counter the group tyranny that was taking place and force the two teams to work on their differences.

Working With Other Teams

As the use of teams expands, more interactions are occurring between teams, causing a number of new issues to surface. Among these are:

- Confusion about which team is doing what work
- Poor communication between teams
- Competitiveness between teams
- Jealousy over which team is getting more perks and recognition
- Lack of responsiveness to the needs of other teams
- Lack of clarity about goals and roles
- Power and control battles
- Personality differences and old stamps

Keeping the team fresh and staying on track requires that the team address these maintenance issues, uncovering the obstacles that often stand in their way:

Obstacles to Effective Team Maintenance

- Unwillingness on the part of the team to learn from past mistakes because of a need to look witty or wise
- Need to present a "pretty" picture to the rest of the organization
- Confusion over who really owns the process and where it is ultimately going
- An existing culture that constantly reminds people of the way things have always been done and that is not tolerant of change
- Distancing from any discussion about maintenance issues by being "too busy" with tasks
- Fear of being out of control, combined with a compulsive need to be in charge

Developing Trust on Teams

Trust has been defined as "the result of creating positive actions over time."[1] It can also be described as the result of a balance achieved between what we give and what we get. When what we give is more than what we get, trust decreases. In order to forgive and trust again, there must be a corresponding increase in what we receive.

Employee mistrust of management was identified in a 1992 study of organizations using self-directed work teams as the number one barrier to teamwork: "Unfortunately most employees are not forgiving. They want to influence their direction, they want constancy of purpose, tactful treatment and recognition for their accomplishments."[2] Trust is now universally recognized as a cornerstone to effective teamwork.

Specific behaviors that increase trust include:

+ Meaning what you say
+ Being involved
+ Not arguing too much
+ Acting consistently
+ Sharing information willingly
+ Showing a willingness to be vulnerable
+ Doing more than what's required
+ Believing that another person has your best interests in mind
+ Being able to ask for help
+ Maintaining a level of honesty that demonstrates personal risk taking
+ Exposing something personal about yourself
+ Acknowledging someone else's skills
+ Taking risks first, before asking others to do so
+ Reaching out to a person distant or different from you

Some people cannot reestablish trust because they are unwilling to forgive past perceived wrongs. The owner of a bookstore turned beet-red trying to convince a team of managers that he had completely forgiven their negative comments about his leadership style. The more he spoke, the more anger oozed out.

In another situation, an employee carefully gave the owner of a business negative feedback about his lack of team attitude and his public criticisms of employees. He calmly took the feedback she presented and thanked her for it. One week later he ripped her apart during her performance evaluation, rating all of her work mediocre. She vowed afterward never to give honest feedback again.

Rebuilding the trust in both these situations will require learning how to forgive. This is not a skill that is commonly discussed in a traditional environment and rarely even in team environments. Yet most people on teams have worked with the same team members for years and have built up attitudes, prejudices, and generalizations that block effective teamwork. Letting go of these blockages will occur when forgiveness has occurred. But forgiving is not easy for many people to do.

The Difficulties in Forgiving

Like listening, forgiving requires practice and commitment to the larger team goal. Sometimes it's hard to let go of grievances, particularly if a power struggle is at the root.[3]

People resist forgiving other people for a variety of reasons, including:

* Viewing total forgiving as somehow agreeing with the wrong done
* Being too proud to forgive
* Believing that forgiveness is a sign of weakness and revenge is a sign of strength

    Q&A #5

* Gaining self-satisfaction from self-pity, whining, and playing the victim
* Hanging on to the familiar feeling of resentment
* Believing that forgiving will increase the chances that the person will hurt you again

Forgiving is not "giving in"; saying "Let's forget it," without explaining how and why, won't work. Forgiving is not denying the incident by saying, "It's no big deal." Too often team members say they forgive when in fact, it's false forgiving.[4]

Five False Ways to Forgive

1. Attaching strings or conditions to the forgiveness
2. Forgiving quickly because there is no real expectation that the person will improve
3. Making a pretense of forgiving but inwardly holding onto the resentment
4. Forgiving only to a point and then no further, as if an arbitrary point could be found
5. Being so distanced from your feelings that you fail to recognize that forgiveness is needed

People at work carry around with them incidents, situations, and stories that remind them constantly not to trust or forgive one another. Sometimes people say, "I don't even know how to forgive this person." Forgiving is a choice—like loving or being happy. Team members can choose to hold on to the grudges or not. If members choose truly to forgive, here is a method that will help.

Step-by-Step Tips on Forgiving

1. Identify the perceived wrongdoing. Describe it in detail (preferably on a piece of paper).
2. Describe in detail your reaction to the wrongdoing. Try to identify as many feelings associated with the wrongdoing as possible.
3. Look at the perceived wrongdoing, and make a conscious decision to forgive what you can forgive (e.g., "I can forgive that she didn't call me later to apologize"; "I can forgive that he made a negative comment about me to my friends").
4. Then decide to forgive the rest. This is the hardest part because it means letting go. Sometimes it helps to consider whether there are any real advantages to hanging on to the last piece of the incident.

People You Need to Forgive

* Anyone you often criticize
* Anyone you feel uncomfortable around
* Anyone about whom you replay harmful scenes over and over
* Anyone you scheme and plan to seek revenge against
* Anyone you allow to have a negative impact on your other relationships

How to Say "I'm Sorry"

Sometimes we know we are the ones who have to ask for forgiveness. Perhaps we talked behind a team member's back, ridiculed one of her ideas, or shared confidential information with another person. Not only is it important to state the wrong we did; it's also important to ask the other person for forgiveness. It allows the balance between the give and the get to be reestablished. One important tip to remember: don't say, "Can you forgive me?" because the person will most likely be thinking, "Of course, I *can* forgive you but it doesn't necessarily mean I will." Instead, ask, "Will you forgive me?" Practice with these statements:

* "Laughing at you during the meeting was hurtful. I wish I hadn't done it. Will you forgive me?"
* "I spoke sharply to you yesterday afternoon. I'm sorry. Will you forgive me?"
* "I talked with someone else instead of you about a problem I have with the team. I apologize for not being direct. Will you forgive me?"

As we discussed in Chapter 4, an apology includes a specific acknowledgment of the behavior, an expression of regret for the behavior, and an offer of restitution. It isn't enough to say, "Sorry."

Surfacing and Resolving Interpersonal Conflicts

Conflict is inevitable with teams. It represents a diversity of thinking. Teams that resolve conflict successfully do so because they expect personal differences and learn how to confront issues, not people. It's important to acknowledge that conflict exists; conducting business as usual when a team is having a conflict reinforces dysfunctional patterns of behavoir, including conflict avoidance.

Factors That Contribute to Team Conflicts

- Lack of training in negotiation and conflict resolution skills
- Inability to speak frankly and without fear of repercussions
- Use of inflammatory statements due to a lack of interpersonal skills
- Conflict avoidance (often as a result of childhood experiences)
- Lack of desire to change
- Past work-related incidents and negative experiences with conflict resolution
- Uncertainty about the future
- Desire to keep everything the same

A self-directed team squabbled over everything. When one member went out and purchased an answering machine for the team with his own money, the team members, rather than being appreciative, got upset that he hadn't asked them first. It's important to remember that people argue, whether it's justified or not.

Why Do People Argue on Teams?

- Different personality styles
- Work-related stress
- Ignorance of who is responsible for a specific task
- Different ideas about what needs to be done
- Similar wants or needs that compete with each other
- Lack of procedures
- Difficulty keeping in touch with one another (different shifts)
- Size of the team
- "Bumps" to the ego
- Anger related to a need that is not being met

The conflict about the purchase of the answering machine didn't end there. Members of the team went to the team manager to complain, and he joined in the fray, objecting to the team member's spending his own money.

What Causes Conflict to Escalate?

* Loyalty to a particular subgroup within the team
* Support from friends within the team, creating factions or polarizing subgroups
* Incompatible potential solutions to conflicts
* Importance of the issue to individual team members
* Members who see themselves as under attack
* Cultural conditioning that admires displays of anger or stubbornness
* Lack of authority to restrain hostile behavior
* The perceived impact of losing

For weeks the answering machine remained a bone of contention, as sides were drawn and swords rattled.

Barriers Used to Keep From Resolving Conflicts

* Justifying the behavior
* Denying that there is a problem
* Allowing hurt feelings to prevent communication
* Launching personal attacks
* Displaying apathy as a way of not addressing the anger or hurt
* Demanding concessions as a condition of working on the problem
* Threatening separation as a way of making others give in
* Making concessions to keep people happy without resolving the original conflict

As tension over the answering machine escalated, the team finally recognized the need to surface the conflict and begin effective resolution. It is necessary to agree on certain principles regarding conflict resolution before discussion begins.

Effective conflict resolution:

• Requires a problem-solving approach
• Seeks to find a wise outcome
• Forces the problem—not friendship and trust—to be the issue[5]
• Recognizes and understands emotions; makes emotions explicit and legitimate
• Focuses on common interests; recognizes that the most powerful interests are basic human needs (security, belonging, recognition, control)
• Defines goals both sides can agree on
• Recognizes that a problem can have more than one solution
• Avoids extreme demands
• Lets both parties emerge as winners
• Sorts areas of agreement from areas of disagreement
• Encourages assertive behavior from all parties

The Three Phases of a Conflict Situation

1. Preparation phase
   • Define the most important issue you are having with the situation. Ask, Why am I frustrated with this situation?
   • Define what you need, not what you are trying to achieve in the situation.
   • Identify who is affected by the conflict and who has control in the situation.
   • Choose your focus by identifying whether the conflict is external, organizational, or interpersonal.
2. Discussion phase
   • List three or four issues in the conflict.
   • Make a list of each person's basic needs in the conflict. Do not state specific goals. Look for common issues.
   • Identify who is affected and who's influencing the conflict. Indicate their degree of control in the situation.
   • Identify common goals that both sides can agree to.
   • Brainstorm solutions that will meet the goals.
   • Develop specific action plans by listing the activities that each person will do, and determine deadlines.
3. Follow-Up Phase
   • Evaluate progress.
   • Offer each other assistance.

Four Tools for Shifting From Negative to Positive Paradigms About Conflict

1. *Reframing.* Require the team to make a conscious effort to identify and reverse its negative attitude.
2. *Shifting shoes.*[6] Require the team consciously to take on the other member's point of view ("If I were this person, why would I be taking such a strong stand right now?").
3. *Affirmations.* Require the team to make positive statements about something they want to be true.
4. *Skill development.* Use periodic team meetings to work on conflict resolution skills.

When tensions arise on a team, members typically have a fight-flight-or-freeze response. This instinctive reaction is an emotional response to the situation. Only after the member processes the emotion and reaches a rational stage can the response shift to assertiveness. In the meantime, all types of aggressive and passive behavior are exhibited.

Aggressive Responses in Conflict Situations

- Hollering, yelling, shouting
- Sneering or making ugly faces
- Physically getting in another person's space
- Arguing a position without stopping
- Interrupting
- Pointing a finger or pen at another person
- Glaring or eyeballing someone
- Using name calling and other put-downs
- Using threats and ultimatums
- Making "you"- or other accusatory statements
- Throwing things; slamming doors, drawers
- Using battle terminology and pounding the table
- Swearing

Passive Responses in Conflict Situations

- Pretending everything's okay
- Running away by getting busy with something else
- Giving in

* Clamming up and not participating
* Acting timid, shy, or withdrawn
* Putting energy elsewhere
* Procrastinating
* Triangling (talking to a third party about another person)
* Backstabbing and name-calling behind a person's back
* Leading a person to make a mistake by withholding needed information
* Being overly helpful and then holding a grudge
* Giving up one's own space
* Making "me"- or other victim statements
* Speaking in an extremely quiet, almost unintelligible voice
* Fiddling with keys, coins, or paper clips as a distracting maneuver
* Having an attitude; pouting and sulking
* Avoiding all eye contact
* Engaging in "under-the-table" comments, eye motions, and gestures designed to express disapproval
* Making statements full of innuendo (double meanings)

Unlike aggressive and passive behavior that occurs automatically, assertive behavior must be practiced and learned. It requires exerting self-discipline over the passive and aggressive responses and instead using assertive techniques to handle the situation.

Assertive Behaviors in Conflict Situations

* Speaking calmly in low voice
* Controlling one's emotional response
* Listening attentively; rephrasing and asking good questions
* Delaying judgment until the topic has been explored
* Being able to put forth one's own viewpoint
* Suggesting alternatives to help reach agreement
* Displaying a confident, open, and friendly manner
* Giving others the benefit of the doubt
* Offering prompt forgiveness of others' wrongdoing
* Being helpful
* Acknowledging mistakes

♦ Being clear about one's own position
♦ Willingness to present opposing viewpoint
♦ Containing physical gestures within one's own space
♦ Showing open palms and making friendly gestures

An accounting manager approached a team member who had purchased lunches for the entire team as a reward and asked why the member had also purchased a lunch for a person outside the team. The team member responded, "Well, he really helped us with the project." The accounting manager replied, "Next time buy lunches only for the people I say can have lunches." The team member said nothing to the manager at the time. However, when he brought the issue up two weeks later at a team meeting, one of the team members remarked that he was obviously still feeling angry and suggested that he speak with the manager directly. The team member responded, "Oh, I'm not angry. I'll just never buy any lunches for anybody ever again." We all have ways of covering up our anger; most of them are counterproductive to effective teamwork.

Three Common Ways of Mishandling Anger

1. *Covering Up Anger*
   ♦ *Giving in regardless of the cost* (saying "No, no it's not a problem. Just take anything you want.")
   ♦ *Collecting injustices* (recalling verbatim incidents that happened five and ten years ago)
   ♦ *Acting silent and sullen* ("The Look") (giving people the silent treatment and, when asked what's wrong, saying, "Nothing.")
   ♦ *Being negative, critical, and sarcastic* (criticizing most of the ideas and suggestions of other members; never being satisfied; like Chicken Little, expecting that any day the sky will fall)
   ♦ *Being passive-aggressive* (exhibiting aggressive behavior in passive ways by pouting, being stubborn, procrastinating, and deliberately taking oppositional points of view)
        During a training session with a small partnership team, it became obvious that one of the partners always

took an opposing point of view. Every time the team got close to a decision, this partner objected and brought the discussion to a virtual halt. This happened again and again, until the other team members began to see the pattern and became assertive enough to address it.

2. *Repressing anger*
   • Convincing oneself there are no angry feelings
   • Collecting and gathering anger but not doing anything about it
   • Exhibiting the anger in physical ways (insomnia and other stress-related responses)

   Team members often let tension build to a point of confrontation and then explode at the other person, making any meeting with both people a hostile event.

3. *Being openly angry*
   • Displaying constant tension and anger
   • Staying at the explosion point
   • Having occasional outbursts of violent temper

One team member would sit in meetings and, as time went on, begin to twitch. He'd shake his head, push his chair in and out, and periodically whack the table. Finally, he'd explode, "That's it! I've had it!" The rest of the team cowered in fear over his anger. It took months before the team was willing to address his behavior.

Typical Problems in Conflict Encounters

• Conflict is confrontational and stressful; adrenaline flows and people's judgment is impaired.
• Conflict is spontaneous and therefore responses are not well planned.
• One person is more or less in control at any given point; sometimes control shifts back and forth from person to person.
• One person typically assumes a defensive position; there is a tendency to blame others.
• One's own position becomes the only possible solution.
• Neither side listens to the other before responding.

- Both sides make quick, subjective judgments.
- Both sides tend to censor their behavior, causing guarded feelings and reactions.
- People have varying levels of skills for handling interpersonal tension.
- Preconceived assumptions about the other person's position block open sharing.
- The encounter accomplishes nothing except to generate more hard feelings.

Harriet Goldher-Lerner in *The Dance of Anger*[7] suggests that most people overfunction in these tense situations, not because they fear the anger and fighting but because they fear that by making the other person uncomfortable, they will be left standing alone, separate from the team. In order to avoid this separation, they overfunction (smooth over the conflict, do more than their share) and allow the other person to underfunction.

When a team can acknowledge its difficulty with conflict and begin to acquire and practice new language skills, the number of conflict situations will be reduced. The first step is for team members to learn a new approach for surfacing problem behavior as it occurs rather than letting it build up. The RISC and the PAUSE strategies and the Matthew Rule help team members structure their opening and responding remarks and their efforts at resolving issues. (Additional conflict resolution strategies are discussed in detail in my book *The Team Building Toolkit*.[8])

The RISC Strategy

When we need to ask another team member for a behavior change, the RISC strategy is a useful tool to help manage the information in specific, behavioral terms.[9]

Step 1.   Report the behavior in specific terms.

Do: Describe exactly what you heard or saw.
Use specific detail.

Don't: Speculate about others' motives or feelings.
Generalize or use stereotypical statements.

Express judgment or condemnation about others' actions or motives.

Example: "Yesterday at our team meeting, you said, 'Oh, Jenny not that stupid idea again!' "

Step 2. State the *impact* the member's behavior had on you.

Do: State your feelings and reactions.
Act in a calm and controlled manner.
Focus on behavior, not the person.
Avoid characterizing the other person as wrong.

Don't: Minimize or negate your own feelings.
Shout, point fingers, holler.
Put down the other person.
Blame.

Example: "I get upset when you make cutting remarks like that, and then I don't want to contribute any more ideas."

Step 3. *Specify* what behavior you would prefer.

Do: Identify what you want the other person to do or not do.
Be specific and complete.

Don't: Use qualifiers ("maybe," "a little bit").
Expect the person to be a mind reader.
Expect big changes overnight.

Example: "I prefer that you just say you'd rather do a different plan and not call my ideas stupid."

Step 4. *State* the positive and negative consequences if the person does or doesn't respond.

Do: State the positive consequences first.
Also state the negative consequences.
Be specific and realistic.

Don't: Exaggerate the rewards or penalties.
Avoid stating strong consequences.

Example: "I'd really like for the two of us to be able to get along as team members. However, if your remarks continue, I will bring my needs to the team for their help."

While the speaker needs RISC to format what he or she wants to say, the listener needs to use PAUSE—a companion process—to respond.

The PAUSE Model

The PAUSE model can be used to handle the interaction as the parties discuss their conflict.

Step 1. Phrase or paraphrase the objection. Also ask the other person to rephrase insensitive statements if necessary.

Example: "Let me make sure I understand what you're saying, Jenny. You heard me call your idea stupid?"

Step 2. Ask questions for more information or elaboration. Focus questions on *what, who, where, when,* and *how.*

Example: "When did I make that comment?" "What had we been talking about during the meeting?"

Step 3. Use time to ask yourself whether you are prepared to respond right away or need time to cool down and sort your thoughts.

Example: "Jenny, I think I'd like to try to recall the incident myself, and then we can talk later this afternoon if that's all right with you."

Step 4. Summarize agreement to close.

Example: "Let me make sure that I understand that at this point we both agree to meet this afternoon to talk more about the incident."

Step 5. Evaluate your response and how you will proceed.

Other Tips:

* Let the person finish presenting the issue before interrupting.
* Ask that insensitive statements be rephrased.

- If the statements can't be rephrased, ask for them to be withdrawn.
- Correct faulty information if you have facts to support your interpretation.
- Clarify vague or manipulative statements (e.g., "What did you mean by that comment?").
- Do not allow assumptions to enter into the discussion.

The Matthew Rule

Many teams have adapted the Matthew Rule (from Matthew 18: 15–17) for handling personal conflicts between team members.

Step 1. Discuss the problem with the team member directly. Ask for a convenient time to meet. Cite the problem without accusation. Express willingness to solve the problem.

Step 2. Bring another team member with you if the first discussion is not successful.

Step 3. Bring the member before the team if the first two discussions are not successful.

Step 4. If results at the team meeting are unsatisfactory, refer the problem to the regular management disciplinary process.

Handling Difficult People

One of the characteristics of difficult people is that they don't recognize that they are difficult. As a consequence, the strategies we have outlined for conflict resolution often do not work with them; they do not recognize their problem behavior as a problem. Consequently, the team ends up trying to manage the difficult person without addressing the behavior directly. Sometimes the employer is one of the difficult people, and surfacing the behavior poses a risk to everyone.

Characteristics of Difficult People

- They are blind to how their behavior affects others.
- They have defects in their feedback systems, so they do not hear what is being said to them.

- They are malcontent and typically always find something wrong.
- They have a desperate need to prove that they are right.
- They are not inhibited by civilizing influences (e.g., help/hinder lists).

Interacting With Difficult People

- Before beginning any conversation with a difficult person, put on your psychological armor. Close all the doors to your personal self and agree to leave the person's cutting remarks and hurtful comments "out in the street."
- Set a specific appointment time to talk about a problem. This lets the difficult person know you are serious.
- Tell your version of how things seem to you. Speak with confidence. Do not yell, fight, or be sarcastic. If necessary, read from prepared notes.
- Be prepared to be dumped on. Know your personal boundaries and maintain your "wall" to prevent the remarks from "getting in."
- Expect to be interrupted. Respond, "Jack, you've interrupted me." Don't be weak.
- Don't explain away everything as the attack begins. Hold firm.
- Don't apologize.
- Paraphrase what is being said. "Let me understand. . . ."
- Ask questions: "What went wrong?" Avoid *why* questions.
- If sniping occurs, smoke out nasty remarks by saying, "I heard a dig; did you mean it that way?"
- Do not mirror any of the behaviors of the difficult person. Stay true to yourself.
- Tell the person what you plan to do. Establish deadlines.
- Remember that your goal is to cope with the person, not to change the person.

QUESTIONS AND ANSWERS:
Building Trust and Resolving Conflicts

1. **Q.** *Why do maintenance issues on the team seem to get worse rather than better as time progresses?*

A. In the early stages of development, most team members are ultrapolite. Discontent is brewing, but no one is brave enough to surface his upset. That takes time. When members do begin to speak up, it's actually a sign that the team is moving along the developmental continuum and is making progress—although it seems just the opposite. Scott Peck in his book *Different Drum* talks about pseudo-community, chaos, emptiness, and then community.[10] The team's middle period reflects that chaos and emptying process. If the team works through its difficulties, the result will be a better feeling of community.

2.   **Q.** *How do you deal with "two-faced" team members who say and act one way in the team meeting and then are totally different outside the meeting?*

A. I hear this complaint probably more than any other. Continue to build the communication skills of the team and try to get team agreement that, by a certain date, members will consciously begin to use the new tools. If someone reverts to the old behavior, team members can gently remind the person of the new approach. The important point here is to surface the behavior and develop some consequences if the behavior persists.

3.   **Q.** *When trust has been broken on a team, how do you go about building it back up again?*

A. Breaking trust is quick and easy; rebuilding it is exceedingly difficult. The first step must be an apology and then the corresponding forgiveness. That still doesn't mean that trust will be forthcoming, but it does leave a blank slate on which to write a new chapter in the relationship. If the person truly is sorry, her behavior will change and trust will be renewed over time as the old behavior is not repeated.

4.   **Q.** *What's the big deal about collecting stamps? Isn't it just a way to describe an accurate judgment about whom you can and can't trust?*

A. Stamp collecting means always having a hidden agenda going on in your head whenever you're talking to other people. You may be trying to get even or to send a hidden message. Your behavior is never clean and open. When that happens among seven to ten people in a room, nothing that is being said means anything and what is not being said means everything. A team with many stamps is crippled in its work.

5. **Q.** *What happens if you apologize for some action and the other person refuses to forgive?*

A. That does happen. I think it means the timing is off; the apology occurred before the aggrieved person was able to say all that he or she needed to say. Let the person vent some more, apologize again, and then give the situation a quiet time. Most likely, the person will respond after his emotions have settled down.

6. **Q.** *After a conflict with a team member, I wrote him a note asking for meeting. He agreed, and we talked through the situation. It resolved that incident, but I still find it hard to work with him. Is this a stamp?*

A. I'm not sure whether this is continuing to bother you because some things didn't get said the first time that needed to get said or, perhaps, because no agreements were made about changing behaviors. I suggest going back to the team member and telling him you're still having difficulty. I know this is hard to do, but real team building requires that we struggle to do what is uncomfortable rather than staying in our comfort zone. In addition, this time make sure you both identify some specific behaviors you are willing to commit to to improve your relationship.

Notes

1. Liz Teal, presentation at the University of North Texas Center for the Study of Work Teams Fall Conference, 1994.

2. "Getting Past the Top 10 Barriers to Successful Self-Directed Teams," *Total Quality* (September 1993): 4–5.

3. Christopher Blake, *Concerned Communications* (Siloam Springs, Ark.: 1992), pp. 5–6.
4. Ibid., p. 7.
5. William Urey and Roger Fisher, *Getting to Yes: Negotiating Agreement Without Giving In* (New York: Penguin Books, 1983).
6. E. Russo and Matthew Eckler, *Mastering Conflict* (King of Prussia, Pa.: Organizational Design and Development, 1995).
7. Harriet Goldher-Lerner, *The Dance of Anger* (New York: Harper & Row, 1985).
8. Deborah Harrington-Mackin, *The Team Building Tool Kit* (New York: AMACOM, 1994), pp. 64–72.
9. Adapted from training materials developed by Professional Resources, Inc., of Herndon, Va.
10. M. Scott Peck, *The Different Drum: Community Making and Peace* (New York: Simon and Schuster, 1987).

6

Improving Team Problem Solving and Decision Making

The real value of a team is found when a group of minds is able to work on a problem, brainstorm ideas, wrestle with options, and, in the end, create or improve something. Nothing else can generate the same level of energy and commitment among a group of people toward an end result.

However, our education system has not equipped team members with the skills needed to achieve group problem-solving and decision-making. In fact, just the opposite is true; our system encourages the development of individual capability, not group skill. No fourth-grader is allowed to say, "Hey, Joe, you're good at word problems, and I'm good at multiplication tables, so let's get together on this test." Yet, that is what we're expecting to have happen in the workplace.

Not only is group problem-solving an odd practice for many, but the demand to strive for consensus has prompted many heated arguments. "If majority rule is good enough for our government, why isn't it good enough for this team?" Yet, as Tom Adair, a quality circle specialist at a Toyota plant in Georgetown, Kentucky, stated, "We learned that if we didn't do it by consensus, we'd have some people fall by the wayside. When it came time for implementation, they wouldn't support it, maybe they'd even sabotage it."[1]

Teams need many different tools and skills to achieve the

level of problem solving and decision making required in organizations today.

Team Decision Making

Nothing demonstrates the value of being a team as much as the decision-making process. The early frustration of listening to everybody, the discipline required to avoid jumping on the first answer, the energy expressed when agreement occurs—all show the uniqueness of teamwork. A decision that reflects the experience, skills, knowledge, opinions, and *commitment* of all team members is always far stronger than a decision made by one person, even if that person makes what is initially believed to be a quicker, better decision. Tom Landry, the former coach of the Dallas Cowboys, knew the value of consensus when he said, "I'd rather have a second-best decision diligently pursued than a first-best decision lackadaisically pursued."[2] Consensus drives the commitment for follow-through that will never exist in majority or autocratic decision-making.

Q&A
#11

The goal of any team decision-making process is to increase the number of alternatives explored, build more objectivity into the decision-making process, and achieve consensus while valuing individual contributions. Managing agreement is a major component of a mature team. Members learn to test for agreement often and to write down points of agreement as they occur. Well-functioning teams recognize that they need to develop their process skills in order to change input into valuable outputs.

Albert Einstein said, "Problems cannot be solved at the same level of thinking that created them." In fact, team members must go beyond simply understanding one another and reaching a decision everyone can live with to learning how to suspend their own views, loosen their grip on certainty, and emerge as a single entity. Peter Senge, in *The Fifth Discipline,* calls this a "container" where the independent parts come together.[3]

One of the most common questions that comes up with teams surrounds the issue of who is suppose to make decisions. Management often feels uncomfortable approaching decision making as it did before; it is concerned that team members will misread their actions as undermining the team process. Meanwhile, team members are on brand-new turf or, as one member said once, "headed for the cliff with no safety net."

Who Should Make What Decisions?

As a team was developing its decision-making criteria for a solution matrix, members realized that they weren't clear about which decisions should be made by the team, which by management, and which jointly by both. Here is the list they made to guide their process:

Upper Management Decisions

+ Decisions that entail the expenditure of more than certain amounts of money
+ Process changes that require capital expenditure
+ Decisions that change organization-wide policy or goals
+ Decisions that affect customers (e.g., price changes, changes from specifications)
+ Personnel decisions
+ Decision to stop serving a customer
+ Decisions that require bringing in outside resources
+ Decision to change from one supplier of a key product or service to another

Team Decisions

+ Decisions that affect the entire team within the limits of its authority
+ Money decisions within a certain budget limit

Joint Management/Team Decisions

+ Mechanical decisions
+ Customer service decisions
+ Decisions on new processes/techniques

Not only does the team have to discuss where decisions will be made; it also needs to develop a sensitivity to factors that influence their ability to make good decisions.

Factors Affecting Team Decision Making

* *The mood of the team*—Level of self-confidence, attitudes toward each other
* *Facts of life*—Recognizing what is and what isn't within the team's control and accepting those facts
* *Urgency*—The speed at which the decision must be made
* *Goal clarity*—Agreement on the issue to be tackled and the goal to be reached
* *Groupthink*—Willingness of members to avoid a sometimes overriding need to agree with one another and instead to explore new and different options
* *Inhibitions*—The extent to which members feel comfortable about expressing their ideas
* *Fear*—Level of fear on the team about reprisals and about management's tolerance for any mistakes
* *Outside criticism*—Pressure and attacks by outside critics who have a vested interest in the outcome
* *Facts vs. value judgments*—Uncertainty about how to integrate information and values when making a judgment.
* *Clarity of boundaries/limits of authority*—The level of understanding among all those involved about who should be making a decision.

Q&A
#1

Outside criticism has a particularly detrimental effect on teams, especially those in government and non profit agencies that deal with governing boards that speak openly to community members about the team's progress. For example, one municipal quality council team became paralyzed in its decision making when members of the board of selectors made comments about the team's work to neighbors and friends.

Q&A
#2

Keys to Successful Decision Making for Teams

* Members' ability to be open-minded and to explore a topic
* Members' willingness to listen carefully to others' points of view Q&A#2
* Members' ability to find a middle ground or alternatives that can be supported by all team members

♦ Members' avoidance of emphatic statements that shut down discussion
♦ Support from significant outsiders
♦ Members' thinking more in questions than in statements
♦ Use of effective problem-solving tools to aid decision making

One of the questions facing a design team working to clarify its role in the implementation of cellular manufacturing teams was whether the team should be responsible for rewarding and recognizing team achievement. One member emphatically stated, "Absolutely not!" and discussion came to an immediate halt. Minutes later, on another topic, a member said, "You'll never catch me doing that." We explored how the conversation changed as soon as a team member countered with "Why not?" To illustrate how often members were using emphatic statements, we all responded, in unison, "Why not?" when such comments were made. It didn't take long to get the point across that emphatic statements would not be supported by the team.

Before achieving consensus, team members need to find points of agreement. This emphasizes the importance of separating the parts all can agree on first and then using these steps to find agreement on the remainder.

Finding Points of Agreement

♦ Clearly state the various positions being taken.
♦ Require each team member to "walk in the shoes" of the other position so that each person is fully able to articulate the needs, wants, and desires of each position.
♦ As each position is being explored, look for points of common ground. They may occur around areas of communication, process, or end result.
♦ Press the team to look for alternatives acceptable to each person. Consider varying focus, breadth of scope, number of people, value of combining/separating ideas.
♦ Explore the possibilities of using parallel processes rather than linear processes (doing two or more things simultaneously rather than one thing after the other).

Consensus Decision Making

There is still considerable resistance to requiring consensus decision making in teams—ironically, usually from people who are
not members of teams that reject consensus decision making because they believe that the only way to achieve consensus is to
offer a decision that has no substance to it.

Most teams realize that voting to reach a decision divides the
team into winners and losers, and losers get even. The key to
successful team decision making lies in the various tools and techniques the team is able to use to reach consensus. The goal must
be to so ingrain the use of tools into the team meeting process
that they become the natural way of proceeding. Without reinforcement, most teams drop the tools shortly after training is completed.

Variations on Testing for Consensus

Members can be asked periodically to register their feelings about
the topic under discussion. Two possible ways are:

1. Thumbs up—Team members register their agreement
   with thumbs up, their disagreement with thumbs down,
   and neutrality with thumbs horizontal.
2. Stop Light—Team members show green index card for
   agreement or "I can live with the decision," red for disagreement, and yellow for "not sure" or "need more information."

More important than the technique used to show consensus
is the willingness of members to indicate their agreement or disagreement to the facilitator. A facilitator should never have to
work very hard to know what the team members are thinking on
a particular issue.

Team Decision Making Tools

The process of problem solving typically involves six steps:

1. Identify the problem
2. Clarify the problem

3. Evaluate causes
4. Develop alternatives
5. Select solution
6. Implement solution

These tools are designed to be used throughout the process to improve the end results for the team.

The Plan-Do-Check-Act Paradigm

Using the quality Plan-Do-Check-Act (PDCA) tool helps teams structure their problem-solving approaches. Without an approach, teams usually allow the most vocal members to chart the course.

Plan

1. Select the problem/process, and describe the improvement opportunity.
2. Describe the current process.
3. Describe all the possible causes of the problem, and agree on a root cause(s).
4. Brainstorm workable solutions and an action plan, including deadlines for improvement.

Do

5. Implement the solution or change on a small scale first.

Check

6. Gather data, and evaluate the results to determine if the solution is having the intended effect.

Q&A
#6

Act

7. Continue the improvement process by revising the approach and acting on results.

A self-directed team was trying to resolve a disagreement among members about how overtime was allocated. The conversation began to get heated. The process observer waived the help/ hinder list; the facilitator kept saying, "Come on, now. Let's talk this through." As a silent observer, I found it difficult not to call out, "Use your tools! Use your tools!"

Every team must have a set of decision-making tools that help shift the team from subjective, argumentative bullying to constructive problem solving.*

Variations on Brainstorming

There are a number of variations on traditional brainstorming, including:

* *Reverse brainstorming*—List all the things that don't work with a process, system, or product.
* *Forced relationships*—Isolate the parts of a problem; analyze the various relationships of the parts; look for patterns; develop ideas based on the patterns.
* *Slip method*—After freewheeling and round-robin brainstorming, ask people to put a last great idea on a little piece of paper. Without fail, the slip method yields at least one or two more ideas.

The Ringi Method

Ringi is a Japanese decision-making procedure in which a written document is sent from one team member to another. Each member edits the document without any interpersonal contact. Drafts are circulated until no more edits are made. Teams can also assign separate parts of a problem to each subgroup, which prepare an answer for its part of the problem.

Period of Silence

It is sometimes effective to encourage team members to observe a period of silence in which they reflect on what they are really talking about and on what isn't being said. Teams rarely use con-

---

*For additional tools, see *The Team Building Tool Kit*, Chapter 5.

templative silence as much as they could to work through strategies and differences of opinion.

Project, problem-solving, and planning teams need to use all types of brainstorming techniques constantly to develop lists of ideas. Those ideas can be refined, combined, and categorized through multivoting and nominal group technique and then put in priority order. We did this for fun with a team by pretending that the team had $20,000 to spend on anything it wanted. Twenty-five ideas popped out through brainstorming; the team whittled the list down to five categories and then multivoted to put them in priority order. At the end, we asked how many people had ever approached a process this way; none had.

Idea Consolidation and Refinement

Let's suppose that a team has brainstormed and come up with seventy-five ideas to improve customer service on the retail floor. To reduce the number of ideas to a workable number, it can use the following criteria to screen out the less attractive ideas:

- Customer orientation—How will our customers like the idea?
- Time—Can the idea be implemented by the deadline?
- Cost—Is the cost too high?
- Resources—Do we have the necessary resources on hand?
- Culture—Does the idea fit with our culture, our approach?
- Usefulness—Is the idea practical?
- Likelihood of acceptance—How much resistance will the idea face?

After a time, teams get very good at quickly developing criteria or screens for good decisions. Some people always introduce the same criteria, and after a while members just look at the person and the criteria immediately come to mind.

Force Field Analysis

Force field analysis is a technique used to present the positive and negative forces at work in any situation or solution. It forces members to think about all aspects and encourages honest reflection. When the analysis is completed, the team can identify ways to strengthen the driving forces and ways to minimize the restraining forces.

To do force field analysis:

1. Draw a large T on a piece of flipchart paper. On the left side write "Restraining forces"; on the right side write "Driving forces."
2. Brainstorm the external and internal forces that are driving you toward your solution.
3. Brainstorm the external and internal forces that are restraining movement toward the solution.
4. Prioritize the driving forces that can be strengthened.
5. Identify restraining forces that can be removed or changed in some way to allow the most movement toward the solution.

Surfacing Blasphemies

Blasphemies are the negative thoughts and slanders that team members think but do not surface in discussion. For example, the organization may place tremendous value on teams, but then the president chews someone out in front of three other staff people. The discrepancy between reality and what the team thinks should be happening can cause serious problems in decision making; the team gets stuck between what it ought to be and what it is.

To surface blasphemies:

1. Ask team members to write down blasphemies on index cards.
2. Deal out the index cards to all the members. Each member reads aloud the card he or she receives.
3. Try to identify common themes. Decide how many to deal with and what to do with the rest.
4. Ask questions:
   • What is the threat behind the blasphemy?
   • What has allowed it to persist?
   • Why haven't we discussed it before?

- What problems will the blasphemy cause in the present and in the future?
- How is this blasphemy blocking our ability to grow as a team?
- What do we want to do about it?

A cross-functional team was given the task of identifying the organization's values as part of a restructuring process. The team listed all the positive values for the company but in doing so realized that they were just words on a piece of paper. Part of what was blocking belief in the values were the blasphemies—all the occasions when people in the organization had acted contrary to the values. The team went behind closed doors and surfaced all the blasphemies, grouped them into categories, and then shared them with the larger planning team. The blasphemies became part of the force field analysis restraining forces that were affecting the reorganization process.

Interrelationship Diagrams

Interrelationship diagrams[4] help the team identify, analyze, and classify the cause-and-effect relationships that exist and make them central to an effective solution. Members are forced to think in multiple directions rather than in linear fashion.

To create an interrelationship diagram:

1. Agree on the issue or problem to be discussed. Be certain that it is clearly understood by all members.
2. Using affinity or brainstorming, gather all the ideas and place them on cards or notes. Arrange the cards in a circular pattern, leaving as much space as possible to draw arrows. Number the cards for quick reference later.
3. Take each idea—one at a time—and identify the cause/influence relationships between it and all the other ideas. Draw an arrow in the direction of the stronger cause or influence. Each pair must have only one arrow indicating which idea is the stronger cause or influence. Continue for all the ideas.
4. Tally the number of in and out arrows for each idea. The

idea with the highest number of outgoing arrows is a root cause or driver and should be tackled by the team first. An item with many incoming areas is key to the outcome or effect and should be a focus for planning.

5. Draw the final diagram. The interrelationship diagram can be made into a matrix in order to create a more orderly display of all the relationships.

We used the interrelationship diagram (Figure 6-1) to sort a group of negative behaviors that were damaging the team. Before the diagram it seemed as if there were a number of huge problems (e.g., judging, distrust, lack of respect). After diagramming, the team was able to see "judging" and "apathy" as the drivers (most arrows going out) and the others as the effect or result of the judging and apathy.

Variance Analysis

Variance analysis can help determine where problems will occur and what their impact will be.

Figure 6-1. Relationship issue: implementation of cellular teams.

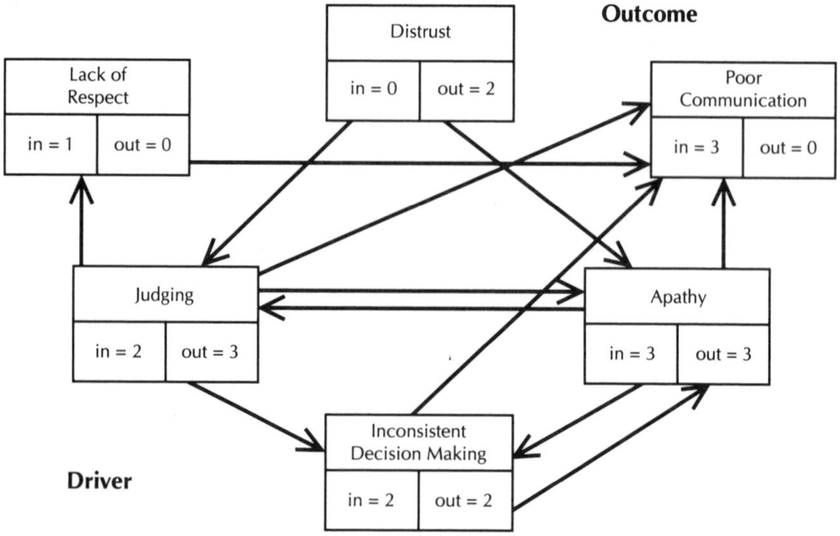

To do variance analysis:

1. List the steps in the solution or process in sequential order.
2. List all the variances that could occur at each step.
3. Create a chart that lists all the variances across the top and all the sequence steps down the side.
4. Match the variances to the steps.
5. Determine which variances cause the biggest problems and focus the team's efforts on eliminating those variances.

Radar Chart

The radar chart is used to make a visual comparison of the gaps between current performance and ideal performance. It clearly displays the important categories of performance and makes strengths and weaknesses very visible.

To construct a radar chart:

1. Select and define rating categories.
2. Identify headers for each of the categories.
3. Define nonperformance and full performance within each category.
4. Draw a large wheel with as many spokes as there are rating categories.
5. Write each rating category at the end of a spoke.
6. Scale each spoke from zero to some scale end point, with "0" at the center equal to "no performance."
7. Rate all performance categories, both individually and as a team.
8. Connect the team ratings for each category, and highlight on the chart.
9. Work on the biggest gap in the most critical category.

The radar chart in Figure 6-2 plots a team assessment that is discussed in depth in Chapter 7.

Figure 6-2. Radar chart.

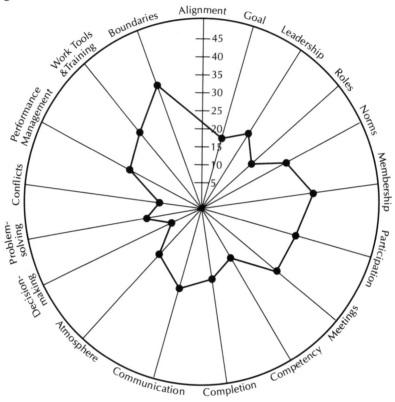

Process Analysis

Process analysis[5] works well to help the team identify the most efficient manner of doing something. By addressing the number of steps involved, minimizing waste, and combining steps wherever possible, the team can increase its efficiency. It is particularly important to complete a process analysis before handing off a task to a team.

To do a process analysis:

1. Select a process done by the team (e.g., scheduling, work orders, progress reports).
2. List the steps involved in the process from beginning to end.

3. For each step identify whether it is an operation (O), transportation (H), unscheduled delay (D) including waiting time, inspection (Q), storage (T), or rework step (R).
4. Identify the amount of time each step takes or the number of people involved. In order to gather data that are reliable, circulate a log to record these steps and the amount of time a task takes.
5. Total the number of steps and the time for each step. Only operation steps add value. All others should be eliminated, minimized, simplified, or combined.
6. Look for ways to do two things at the same time (parallel rather than linear processes) and to collect data once at the source.

A data processing team in a bank used process analysis to reduce the steps in a mailing process from seventeen to eleven. During the discussion, members became more and more motivated to try the new process as they saw it save time and repetitive effort.

Working Toward a Final Decision

Teams often have trouble bringing closure to a debate and reaching a final decision. If the process is well done, the team moves forward; if the process is weak, the team will bring the discussion up over and over again.

The Decision Matrix

A cross-functional management team had been struggling with a decision whether to move ahead on a departmental reorganization plan. The CEO had a definite opinion, and a number of the team members dreaded the upcoming meeting, anticipating a long monologue. To eliminate that possibility, several team members designed a decision matrix (Figure 6-3) listing the following criteria across the top of the paper and the solution choices on the horizontal:

Figure 6-3. Decision matrix.

Decision Criteria

Decision Description

Decision Options

Decision Criteria		
Accomplishes the goal		
Ease of implementation		
Provides flexibility and adaptability		
Able to reach consensus		
Meets deadline		
Supports big picture		
Have all information needed		
Positive impact on productivity/efficiency		
Compatible with company vision		
Strong participation in development		
Cost/return ratio is good		
Confidence of management		
Supports and/or improves quality		
Risk level is acceptable		
Benefits to customer/company		
Able to measure results		
Management effort		
Total Score		

Key: 5 = High
1 = Low

- Should the decision be made by management? (This became the question that always needed to be asked first.)
- Does it accomplish the goal?
- Does it give us flexibility?
- Are we able to reach consensus on this choice?
- Can we meet deadline?
- Does the choice support the big picture?
- Do we have all the information we need on this choice?
- Does the choice have low negative impact?
- Is it compatible with the organization's vision?
- Is this choice easy to implement?
- Does the choice involve everyone when necessary?
- Is the cost/return ratio good?
- Does the team have confidence in the choice?
- Will the choice have no adverse affect on quality?
- Is the risk level low?
- Does this choice give us the ability to meet customer requirements?
- Are the benefits to the company high?
- Are we able to measure results?
- Does this choice provide long-term workability?
- Are sufficient resources available to implement this choice?

The team then weighted each of twenty criteria on a one hundred-point scale. Each member filled in his or her grid for each of the solutions; then the team averaged the scores (a variation of nominal group technique) to achieve a total team score. The scores for the two favored choices were very close, but the team decided neither was high-scoring enough to be selected as the right choice. It ended up blending aspects of both solution options for a third choice that got high scores across the board.

The Paired-Choice Method

When a team has to deal with a large number of different options that are all relatively similar and it wants to keep the steps to a solution as simple as possible, the paired-choice process (comparing one choice to another) (Figure 6-4) can quickly eliminate less attractive options.

Figure 6-4. Determining the best choice.

	Customer satisfaction	Training	New equipment	More pay
Customer satisfaction	▓▓▓			
Training		▓▓▓		
New equipment			▓▓▓	
More pay				▓▓▓

To use this method:

1. List the various decision choices along the top of a piece of paper (e.g., Option 1, Option 2, Option 3, etc.).
2. List the same decision choices in the same order along the side of the paper (e.g., Option 1, Option 2, Option 3).
3. Move across the chart, comparing the first choice to every choice along the top row, one set at a time (e.g., Option 1 vs. Option 2, Option 1 vs. Option 3, Option 1 vs. Option 4).
4. The choice that has the largest number of "preferred" votes wins.
5. If two choices are tied, repeat the process with a shorter list of options.

The Implications Wheel

The futurist Joel Barker coined the phrase "the implications wheel."[6] To use this method, the team places a prospective decision in the center of a circle (see Figure 6-5). Then the team brainstorms on the implications of making a particular decision and writes the implications in circles along spokes radiating from the

Figure 6-5. The implications wheel.

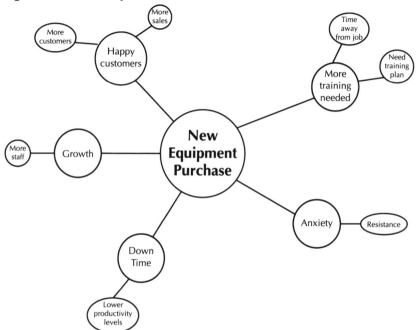

center circle or wheel. Those implications have further implications, which become spokes off the smaller circles, and so on. This tool is particularly effective when developing a vision, product, or service.

Scenario Thinking

Scenario thinking encourages the team to explore "what ifs." It helps the team begin to visualize the outcome of any pending decision and determine if it is a wise one. Scenario thinking is very helpful if a team is working on reorganization and needs to explore outcomes. Steps in scenario thinking include:

1. Determining what can and can't be changed
2. Changing what can be changed
3. Identifying all the points that may seem trivial today but may become significant tomorrow

4. Discussing multiple scenarios by simulating hypothetical situations

The Tree Diagram

The tree diagram (Figure 6-6) is a planning tool for breaking down a decision into detailed action steps. It encourages the team to expand its thinking when creating solutions and allows everyone to check the links and completeness of every level of the plan.

To create a tree diagram:

Figure 6-6. The tree diagram.

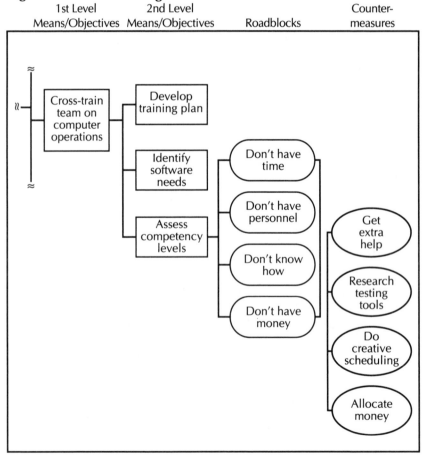

1. Create a clear, action-oriented statement as a goal.
2. Brainstorm the major task areas or "means" by which the goal will be achieved. Use verb phrases for each task header (e.g., measure results, provide recognition).
3. Use Post-Its to move task areas around as the detail emerges.
4. Break each major heading into greater detail. Ask, "What needs to be addressed to achieve the goal statement?" Most trees are broken out to the third level of detail. At each level of detail, ask, "Is there anything obvious we've forgotten?"
5. Working left to right, place the headers in sequence order. Try to identify tasks that have to occur at the same time. Place them together in the same column. When the chart is completed, draw lines between items.
6. Branch likely problems off each step by asking, "What could go wrong?"
7. Identify reasonable countermeasures to offset problems, and branch off each likely problem.

How to Complete the Decision Making

1. Check for understanding among team members about the decision made and why it was made.
2. Communicate the decision to all those affected, including absent team members and members of other departments.
3. Develop an action plan to implement the team's decision (see Figure 6-7).
4. Define process steps in the action plan, the owner responsible for completing each step, and the deadline.
5. Establish a time line, with major milestones identified.
6. Celebrate the success of making a team decision.

Q&A
#7

Questions and Answers:
Improving Team Problem Solving and Decision Making

1. **Q.** *At what point should management step in to make a decision?*

Figure 6-7. The action plan.

To:
From:
Team members:
Subject matter:
Date:

Task	Team Action Person	Start Date	Completion Date	Team Contact Person	Red Alert	Notes

A. Management needs to define its criteria for when it will step in to make a decision and then communicate those criteria to the team before a project begins. The team, of course, can negotiate with management if it sees the situation differently. What doesn't work is for management to give the team decision-making authority and then take the authority back when it doesn't like what the team has done. It always reminds me of entrapment ("I'll wait to see what mistakes you make") and does nothing to build the relationship between management and the team.

2.   **Q.** *What if a team is making lots of wrong decisions?*

   A. The first question is, Why is the team making so many wrong decisions? It's important to determine whether the wrong decisions are a result of competency (skill) issues or conduct (behavior) issues. If the errors are occurring because of lack of competency, additional training and skills coaching are necessary. Sometimes assigning a supervisor to help a team temporarily with technical problems can be of enormous help. If the errors are occurring because of conduct (e.g., team members are unwilling to work through problems, resulting in inaccurate information transfer, missed deadlines, etc.), I suggest asking for time on the team's agenda and addressing the problem directly with specific data.

3.   **Q.** *Our plant manager drops in periodically to participate in our team meetings, and within minutes he has taken over. He immediately says what he thinks needs to happen, and everyone else agrees. How could we change this pattern?*

   A. I've seen teams achieve good results in handling this problem by doing a couple of things. Be sure you have an agenda, a process observer, a timekeeper, and a strong facilitator. Use those tools to get the meeting started and organized. Then use one of the problem-solving tools to think through your decisions. When the manager enters in mid-stream, the team is already engaged in employing its tool, giving him no choice but to work with the tool (and the process) instead of creating his own. You might also find it helpful to have one or two members of the team speak to him directly. Many plant managers don't know how controlling they are. Most are very responsive to suggestions from teams that they back off a bit.

4. **Q.** *What if everyone doesn't know how to use these tools?*

    A. Most people don't know how to use the tools until they put pencil to paper. Usually getting started takes someone's saying, "Look, let's try this tool and see if it helps us get answers to this problem." Once people get use to using the tools, the techniques become second nature. One caution: people shouldn't try to use the same tool for every situation that comes up.

5. **Q.** *Where do you find all these tools?*

    A. The quality management movement has provided a storehouse of tools for problem solving and decision making. Most TQM literature includes such tools. Experiment. Use what works for you. Forget the rest.

6. **Q.** *What about data gathering? Shouldn't a team be doing that, too?*

    A. Absolutely! It's important to measure key processes and things that have real meaning for the team. The method can be as simple as pencil-and-paper charts or as sophisticated as computerized matrices. Most teams need help initially setting up five or six key items to measure and creating the charts and graphs.

7. **Q.** *We don't have any training in problem solving and decision making tools. Where do we begin?*

    A. I'd start with brainstorming, multivoting, and some simple data collection. Then, bit by bit, share more tools with the team. Most teams really like the tools when they see how much they improve the team's decision process and results. They really like to be able to come to management with all their data compiled and good, solid thinking behind their recommendations.

8. **Q.** *Some people can compile data but not explain what it means. They go round and round until everyone is lost. What can you do?*

   A. Compiling and analyzing are two different skill levels. The people you describe probably lack skill in analyzing and synthesizing. I suggest that a supervisor or manager be invited to a team meeting to explain how he or she analyzes and synthesizes data. See if that person can teach the team members a step-by-step thinking process for the particular data your team is reviewing.

9. **Q.** *What do you do if a team is presenting information and you see an error in the data or in the team's thinking? Should you bring it out and say something right there?*

   A. Teamwork is not a game. If an error has been made, it needs to be corrected as quickly as possible, especially if other decisions are dependent on the team's data. If I felt it might be embarrassing for the team, I'd ask for a break and speak to the team's presenter. If that person isn't receptive, I'd go to the meeting facilitator. It's important to be sensitive to people's feelings and to point out the error in a constructive manner; however, it is not correct to allow a team or organization to make a mistake just to let some people save face. For teams to work, they must be prepared to make mistakes and recover from them.

10. **Q.** *When we're brainstorming, there are so many ideas presented that just won't work. Why do we have to waste the time?*

   A. I know it's hard when new people are learning how to think and process information and you've been at it for years. Brainstorming allows those who have never had an opportunity to contribute before to do so. It's to be expected that some of the ideas will be off the mark. The best way to deal with them is to set up your criteria screens ahead of time and then use the screens to filter out the ideas that aren't any good. I caution you, however, that just because an idea didn't work a year ago doesn't mean that it won't work today. A year ago, it didn't make sense for some companies to invest any money in the Internet because there was no activity on it that affected their products. If they were to experiment with the Internet again, they might find lots of prospective customers. You just never know.

11. **Q.** *Is there any way to speed up the decision-making process on a team? It takes forever, and we all lose interest.*

A. Perhaps if the team begins to use some of the tools and sets up a problem-solving protocol or method, the process will go faster. You can also encourage members to learn not to comment on every item or idea that comes up. However, with eight to ten people in a discussion, even something fairly straightforward will take twenty to thirty minutes to resolve.

Notes

1. P. Keith Kelly, *Team Decision-Making Techniques* (Irvine, Calif.: Richard Chang & Associates, 1994), pp. 59–69.
2. Tom Landry and G. Lewis, *Tom Landry: An Autobiography* (New York: Walker and Company, 1991).
3. P. Senge, *The Fifth Discipline* (New York: Doubleday/Currency, 1990).
4. M. Brassard and D. Ritter, *The Memory Jogger* (Methuen, Mass.: Goal/QPC, 1994).
5. J. Harbour, *The Process Reengineering Workbook* (New York: Quality Resources, 1994).
6. Joel Barker, *The Implications Wheel* (Minneapolis, Minn.: Aurora Pictures, 1994).

7

Measuring a Team's Worth

The purpose of a team is to achieve a goal: investigating and streamlining a process, brainstorming solutions to a troublesome production problem, creating value-added product or service. However, many organizations create teams not as part of a new strategic plan but at the drop of a hat because a plant manager, boss, or owner said to do so. As a consequence, the team does not have a strong sense of its purpose other than to please management. Keeping up appearances becomes the goal. After all, who wants to be associated with a team that has disbanded? Other times managers create teams because they think that doing so will be a plus for their performance appraisals. In these situations, team members do not see the need for a team structure to achieve a goal; in fact, members often feel that other structures, such as the old supervisory model, would better serve the group.

Sometimes a team is created, months go by, and team performance begins to drift. Attendance is sporadic, commitment low. The team appears to be treading water, but no one can decide whether to energize or disband the team.

Jack Gordon, the editor of *Training Magazine*, has stated, "The question isn't 'How do we get our teams right so the organization can be more effective?' The question is 'How do we get the organizational system right?' When you get your systems right, you find many situations where teams don't work and others where they do."[1]

Thus a dilemma begins to develop for the organization: does

it stay on the path of the strategic plan to use teams (and ignore the grumblings of disenchanted team members or the mediocre result), or does it take some risk and decide to examine the validity of the team's continued existence and its real worth? Further, how does it do that examination?

The self-directed packaging team in a manufacturing company was faced with this dilemma when members of the team became quite vocal about their desire not to be a team. They had been selected by management because of the nature of their work, not their predisposition to be a team. Their negativity continued throughout the early team-building training as members halfheartedly participated. Their message was always the same: we don't want to be a team. They wanted someone else to take responsibility for the decisions; they wanted a supervisor to be accountable for handling communication with other departments and customers; they wanted management to deal with conflicts. It became necessary to evaluate the team's existence, even though management balked at the possibility of disrupting the strategic plan.

Myths That Interfere With Examining the Team's Progress

It seems somehow sacrilegious to question a team's work, almost as if doing so is being against motherhood and apple pie. So people create a set of myths that keep their assessments soft and ineffective. Among these myths are the following:

- People are causing all the problems on teams, and there is nothing we can do about people.
- More training will solve the team's problems.
- All systems have flaws that cause them not to work well, and so do teams. Examination will make little difference.
- Teams are the right way to structure the modern organization, and we'll just have to bear with the problems.
- If the teams aren't working, we must be doing something wrong. They're working at other places.

♦ Control and accountability are not compatible with empowerment and teams.
♦ Disbanding a team represents failure.

A project team had been given the huge assignment of improving organizational communication. It spent its first year analyzing existing communication—what was good about it, what didn't work. Round and round they went, adding more and more data to the analysis. When it came time for suggesting solutions, the team became paralyzed, and invariably conversation drifted back to gathering more information about the problem. Essentially they were operating under all of the myths we have listed. Part of the improvement process included surfacing the thinking that kept the team stuck and taking the risk of truly evaluating its progress.

Evaluating the Team

Evaluation of a team can range from answering the simple question "How are we doing?" to conducting an in-depth, full reexamination. Other evaluation tools can include:

♦ Benchmarking with other teams in other organizations
♦ Comparing the team's progress against its original goals and time line
♦ Using an outside consultant to observe the team in action and develop a summary of findings
♦ Holding periodic, informal team discussions to explore the pluses and minuses of the team's functioning

Assessing the Team Charter

Reexamination of the team's essential functions must focus on purpose, strategy, roles, people, processes, feedback, and interface with others in the organization—all the elements in the original team charter. There are also a number of key players in the process: the team itself, the resource team (sometimes called a steering committee), the team champion, and the team's customers. (See Chapter 8 for role descriptions.) The team can use a radar chart to plot its scores; see Figure 6-2 for a radar chart.

The reexamination of the charter should occur annually, or more often if problems exist, and should include an in-depth discussion of each of these categories:[2]

Original Problem to Be Addressed

* Does the team approach still make sense strategically for the organization and tactically for the department?
* Are there other approaches that would work just as well?
* Was the team originally created to get around the need to restructure or solve another problem? Is this consideration still relevant?
* Does management still believe that the use of a team is the most effective way to solve this particular problem/concern?
* Does the team assist with accomplishing strategic goals already developed or is the team doing something of little consequence?
* Is the team making a contribution to the larger organizational goals?

Goal(s) to Be Achieved

* Is the team's mission (purpose) still valid?
* Has the team developed specific goals? Are they meaningful to team members? Do team members ask, "Do you want me to do this or my job?" (Such a question is a clear sign that the members' jobs and team responsibilities are not seen as interdependent.)
* Has the team achieved the goals it originally set out to achieve?
* Were the results acceptable?
* Have new goals been identified as old goals are reached? Are all members of the team clear about the new goals?
* How are the goals measured? Are the results shared, or are the goals just words on a piece of paper?
* Are the goals reasonable, or were they too big to begin with?

* Has the team gone off on tangents or pursued individual agendas, rather than working toward the goal?

Key Activities the Team Was Expected to Undertake

* What is the history of the team's progress, and what is its level of ability to do key activities?
* Was the team given too much too quickly?
* Was too little responsibility delegated?
* Did the team receive adequate on-the-job skills training while becoming a team?

Key Results the Team Was Expected to Achieve

* Were clear, measurable standards set from the beginning? Did the team buy in to those measures?
* What have the results been to date?
* Have the benefits of the results been shared?

> Q&A
> #9

Resources Available to the Team

* Does the team have all the work tools it needs?
* How consistent has the application of resources been?
* Has management been an active player in support of the team?
* Has the team champion (see Chapter 8) been an active player?
* Have staff turnover or changes in management personnel affected the distribution of resources?

Type and Frequency of Communication Expected of the Team

* How often has management communicated with the team about "big picture" goals and results?
* Who is communicating with the team on a regular basis now, and what is the emphasis of that communication?
* Do feedback processes exist, and how effective are they?
* How often does management visit the team and/or do regular "walkabouts"?
* Does the team maintain effective communication links with all of its customers inside and outside the organization?

The Nonnegotiables or Boundaries the Team Was Expected to Observe

* Were control mechanisms established in the beginning?
* Are they still valid?
* Has the team observed the boundaries (e.g., no capital expenditures, no changes to facilities, no hiring)?
* Did the team set up boundaries that were never openly agreed to and that as a result inhibited their ability to achieve?

Why Specific Members Were Selected for the Team

* Have all team members been assigned to active roles?
* Have all team members received similar training?
* Do team members understand what they are expected to contribute?
* Do they have confidence in themselves?
* How much turnover has occurred on the team?
* Have replacement members been brought up to speed?

Team's Authority to Make Decisions

* Has delegation of authority been clear and consistent?
* Has too much or too little authority been delegated?
* Have the results of the team been used?

Other Significant Team Roles and Relationships

* Have the significant roles been identified? Are people clear about their specific roles?
* How are others in the organization reacting to the team?
* How are conflicts resolved between different teams and departments?
* Do different teams seem to care about one another?
* Are duties distributed fairly among all team members?

The Time Frame Within Which the Team Was Expected to Work and Key Milestones

* Are expectations about the progress realistic?
* Were short-term end points set up to measure progress?
* Have successes to date been celebrated?

Evaluating the Team's Performance

In addition to compiling anecdotal data as part of its review of its charter, the team needs to create hard-data measurements of its progress.

Most teams need help deciding what to measure and how to do it. The coach is invaluable in this process. Measures should be kept simple and provide real numbers that team members believe in. Four or five simple charts should provide the data necessary for the team to decide if it's accomplishing its goal.

Sample Measures of Team Performance

Q&A
#7

+ Process yield coupled with reduced cycle time
+ Quality (mean time between failures)
+ Number of reports generated within specified time frame
+ Profits
+ Cycle time
+ Work-in-progress inventory
+ Percentage of inventory accuracy
+ Percentage of location accuracy
+ Production costs
+ Customer satisfaction
+ Number of customer orders entered/invoiced in day
+ Responsiveness to customer inquiries (number of requests received and processed)
+ RGAs processed (number within specific time frame)
+ Orders processed (taken and entered)
+ Order entry accuracy (number of errors)
+ Number of information requests processed
+ Telephone efficiency (number of rings)
+ Telephone frequency (number of calls made and received)
+ Invoicing accuracy (percentage correct)
+ Percentage of shipping accuracy
+ Downtime (number of hours)
+ System enhancement (list of requests made and processed)
+ Courtesy (conformity to team norms)
+ Housekeeping
+ On-time delivery

* Receiving performance (percentage of daily correct)
* Efficiency as a comparison of work to waste

One technique that works particularly well is for the team to identify six to eight performance measures. Individual members of the team then take responsibility for conducting the different measurements and reporting the results at the weekly team meeting. For example, inventory accuracy may be defined as the accuracy with which the member locates a specified number of items on a given day. The results are shown as an average percentage against the goal. All the results from the individual reports are then compiled for a weekly team total.

The review of the team charter and the team performance data is best done as a team effort, with all members contributing their perceptions about the progress made so far. The process observers (the member of the team assigned the task of monitoring the team's help/hinder list and letting the team members know when they are not behaving as the list requires) must play an active role in keeping discussion open, honest, and direct. Analyzing the team charter lets the team know when glitches occurred, either in its original concept or in its early formation, that are continuing to impact the team's performance.

A customer service team conducted an analysis of its original charter and realized that it had never been given clear authority to end a relationship with a customer. Members believed that it was okay to hang up the phone on an abusive customer. When the team met with management to discuss the limits of its authority, it became clear that the right to terminate a relationship with a customer was a management prerogative and that the team's authority was limited to passing the problem on to a supervisor or manager.

Evaluating the Team's Effectiveness

After reviewing the charter, the team continues with an assessment of the amount of progress it has made toward achieving tasks and of the team's overall effectiveness. Team members can perform a self-assessment by measuring the following individual and team skills: knowledge of duties, level of motivation, role clarity, amount of experience and training, level of skill in communication, cooperation, and coordination, and development of new interteam relationships.

Many teams find it difficult to take the time to evaluate their progress in anything but the most general terms. Yet evaluation is critical to the growth of the team. It works best to designate a particular time (e.g., every four months) and to use a predesigned format.

Measuring Task Progress

- Are team members competent to perform all relevant tasks?
- Are all tasks performed according to standard?
- Does the team utilize the material resources provided in order to perform the tasks?
- Are adequate time and staff allocated to do the job well?
- Does the team gather and use all information needed to perform the task?
- Does the team demonstrate the ability to plan and organize tasks?
- Does the team demonstrate the ability to generate and try new approaches?
- Does the team respond to the appropriate rewards and recognition given it?

Judging Team Effectiveness

- Are all team members committed to working hard together?
- Can each team member clearly identify the vision, mission, goals, and values of the team?
- Has the team established an effective rotating leadership system?
- Does the team meet regularly to work on projects and other team-related tasks? Are meeting roles shared?
- Do team members express feelings of unity?
- Do members demonstrate a willingness to take on responsibility for the team's success as a whole?
- Are there feelings of trust and support among members?

- Are conflicts handled in a way that brings the problem out in the open and encourages communication until resolution occurs?
- Are members willing to share and use feedback?
- Do team members express personal and team satisfaction with the results?

The team then combines the assessment of its original charter with the focused assessment of task process and team effectiveness and determines if continued work is warranted.

The bakery team in a specialty shop had been calling itself a team for three years, but close examination of the charter, task process, and team effectiveness showed that, in fact, the team didn't act like a team at all. The team leader had become the de facto supervisor, meetings were nonexistent, the team goal was old and forgotten. Recommitment to functioning as a team meant answering the questions, carefully identifying what needed to change, and developing an action plan to get the team back on track.

Bringing Customers Into the Evaluation Process

The purpose of a team's work is to satisfy a customer, whether internal or external. For a team to know whether it is succeeding, it must ask its customer for feedback. A customer satisfaction index, which consists of a set of specific measures or questions, is particularly effective for eliciting comments from internal customers, because they have more time and willingness to participate in the feedback process.

A number of teams use a customer-service index to help their customers rate the quality of the teams' work. Questions typically relate to quality, problem solving, scheduling, and communication. When the product is delivered, the customer team completes the index form. If for some reason the customer inspection reveals that the product is shoddy and contains a defect, the customer team assumes responsibility for dealing with the problem. Supplier teams are allowed to reject a customer index rating if the problem is not sufficiently described.

A customer service team developed a customer satisfaction scoreboard—a bulletin board that recorded key data every day. When a large account came in, the team rang a large cow bell that brought all the members together to celebrate the success. Three minutes later they were back at work.

360-Degree Evaluations

The relatively new process of conducting 360-degree performance evaluations encourages feedback about the team from many different people both inside and outside the organization. Internal and external customers, team members, managers—anyone who has significant interactions with the team—contribute to the evaluation process.[3] To structure the 360-degree evaluations, a number of questions must be answered:

+ How many raters should be involved? (generally between five and ten)
+ Who should do the rating? (a collection of internal and external customers is preferable)
+ Who has ultimate responsibility for the appraisal? (typically the supervisor or team leader)
+ How is the appraisal conducted? (often a coach is selected with a few other people acting as objective advocates)
+ How are raters selected? (at random from a pool).

There are several cautions with 360-degree evaluations. First, external customers often don't want to be involved in rating teams. It's best to use existing customer data whenever possible. Second, other teams typically don't like to give negative feedback about their peers for fear of retaliation. It's best to accumulate the feedback data over time looking for trends or patterns by using the following criteria:

+ Did the team follow up on problems, decisions, and requests in a timely manner?
+ Were expectations and needs clearly communicated?
+ Was information shared in a way that was helpful?

+ Did the team establish a plan to meet future needs of customers, management, and others?
+ Did the team adhere to all schedules and deadlines?
+ Were problems (if they occurred) resolved in an open and courteous manner?

Tips for 360-Degree Evaluations

+ Provide guidelines or examples to encourage specific rather than vague or generalized feedback.
+ Keep the report form short (five to fifteen questions, one or two pages in length).
+ Provide raters with the option of being identified or remaining anonymous.
+ Institute a rule that prevents raters from including a negative comment on the evaluation without speaking to the team beforehand.

Continuing a Team's Charter

After conducting a thorough assessment and receiving an evaluation from its customers, the team is ready to sign up for another "tour of duty." The team charter should be revised to reflect current realities. New goals should be set, resources reassigned, and so on. Unlike the first charter that was created by management or a steering committee, this charter should be the work of the team, with input from management. This is also a good time to change roles, bring in new members, assign a new team champion, or address unacceptable team behavior.

Closing Out a Team

All involvement processes, including teams, have a natural birth, life, and death cycle. A team should be closed out when:

+ The work originally assigned has been completed and results have been checked against original goals and customer needs

- The results originally expected have not been achieved after much work and effort
- Personality conflicts are extreme and dysfunctional behavior has made it impossible for the team to work together

The assessment process may lead to the conclusion that the team is not the most effective way to proceed or that the task has been completed and the team needs to disband. If this is the case, it may be helpful to consider these points:

- Whenever possible, allow the team to reach this conclusion on its own, through the assessment process.
- All change results in feelings of loss. Allow the team time to process its feelings. Identify the team's gains and the losses.
- Clearly identify the team's accomplishments and provide a way to celebrate them.
- Review the collaborative process and identify what worked and what didn't.
- Establish responsibility for monitoring the results over time.
- Identify any remaining tasks to be done.
- Communicate the change in status to everyone affected.
- Recognize each member's achievements and his or her individual value.
- Identify the lessons learned along the way.

The CEO of a company didn't want a team to feel badly as it was disbanding, so he took the team to lunch and then proceeded to inflate the results of its work. As he talked on and on, the team became confused about why it was disbanding if in fact it was so terrific. Later, when he failed to use any of its work, the team experienced loss all over again. It is better to let the team experience the appropriate feelings and then move on.

At a large engineering firm, teams work for twenty weeks and then display their accomplishments in a "science fair" fashion. The steering committee then decides whether the team has finished its tasks or needs another ten- to twenty-week extension.

QUESTIONS AND ANSWERS:
Measuring a Team's Worth

1. **Q.** *Are there particular assessment tools that can help teams evaluate their performance?*

   A. Yes. Here are some that we've found to be particularly effective:

   Campbell-Hallam Team Development Survey (719) 633-3891

   Employee Empowerment Survey (Talico) (904) 241-1722

   Group Process Questionnaire and Meeting Effectiveness Questionnaire (Aviat) (313) 663-2386

   Superior Team Development Inventory (4 parts) (HRD Press) (800) 822-2801

   Skillscope (Center for Creative Leadership) (910) 545-3756

   Team Leadership Practices Inventory (James Kouzes and Barry Posner, Pfeiffer & Company) (619) 578-5900

   Team Strength Performance Assessment (Tercon) (800) 877-4776

   TeamView/360 (Pfeiffer) (800) 274-4434

   The Team Effectiveness Profile and What Makes Your Team Tick? (Organizational Design and Development) (215) 279-2002

   The Team Review Survey (Dave Francis and Don Young, Pfeiffer & Company) (619) 578-5900

2. **Q.** *How often should a team evaluate itself?*

   A. Teams need to evaluate themselves on a regular basis. In the early stages, a team should conduct a brief evaluation every two or three months just to be certain it is on track. Later, conducting a six-month evaluation will help the team spot trouble and realign itself quickly. What doesn't work is to do nothing in the way of evaluation for one or two years and then start criticizing the team's results. In many ways, it's best to follow the process that works best for individual performance evaluations and adapt it for the team.

3. **Q.** *What if the team thinks it should keep going but management disagrees?*

A. That's a tough one. The team could certainly ask management what results it would have to achieve to be allowed to continue and then ask for a "window of time" in order to prove itself. However, ultimately management has the authority to decide whether there will or won't be teams.

4. **Q.** *Would you evaluate a self-directed work team differently from a project or problem-solving team?*

   A. Self-directed teams have a longer lifespan than project or problem-solving teams. They also have many more interpersonal issues that have to be resolved because the team works together constantly. They may need more time to be effective than project teams. However, the other evaluation elements—including the charter and customer feedback—should be the same.

5. **Q.** *Why do people take it personally when someone suggests that the team should be disbanded?*

   A. It's natural to feel a sense of loss when a team is disbanded. Members have spent considerable time together, and now there is a void. Many people derive some of their identity and their sense of well-being from being a part of a supportive team in the workplace. When the job is done, they want to create new jobs to keep the team going. We have to make it more than okay for a team to close.

6. **Q.** *We don't have time to go through a lengthy review process. Isn't there some "quick and dirty" process we could use?*

   A. The one that works best for us is to do a quick check on goals, roles, and procedures. Do clear and measurable goals exist for the team? Are roles delineated and agreed upon? Are adequate team procedures in place? Usually if problems exist, they'll surface with one of these three questions. But we still encourage the use of the more in-depth assessment to understand the team's problems.

7. **Q.** *We're still using the old performance evaluation forms with people on teams. Is that wrong?*

A. The traditional performance evaluation form focuses on individual achievement. Factors such as initiative, leadership,
and independence are not valid measures in a team environment. Also, many people separate their team tasks from their
regular work. Continued use of the old evaluation tool reinforces the idea that people have two different jobs (their job
on a team and their real job). When the evaluation form
doesn't include any assessment of the work on teams, it's not
surprising that people weigh their real job more heavily.

Many organizations are in the process of redoing their
team evaluation processes. It is appropriate to incorporate
team participation on the performance evaluation form.

8. **Q.** *What if management's perception of the team's progress and
the team's perception differ?*

A. Sometimes that happens, especially if the expected results
were not clear or measurable from the beginning. I think
management has an obligation to let the team present its case
for continuance. A team that fights to stay alive is one I would
want to keep regardless of its task.

9. **Q.** *What if team results are never measured?*

A. As someone once said about goal setting, "If you don't know
where you're headed, how will you know when you get
there?" I encourage the team to begin to count—almost anything—and track the count over time. There will come a day
when someone asks what the team has accomplished or why
the team should continue to exist.[4] That's when it's great to
have the data to present.

10. **Q.** *Should a well-functioning team remain intact after reaching
the goal, or should there be a change in the players when a
new project is assigned? Do you run the risk that the team
will get too comfortable?*

A. I don't think there is a black-or-white answer to this one. Just
because a team reaches its goal doesn't mean that it should
get a complete overhaul. In fact, that could be perceived as

punishment for doing a good job. On the other hand, the completion of a project is a natural time to change members. To avoid the team's getting too comfortable, it's important for members to have short-term, realistic goals.

11. **Q.** *What if one team member sees a need to evaluate how the team is handling procedures and the rest of the team members are content with the status quo? What does the team member do?*

  A. There is not much any one team member can do if seven or eight others disagree. However, there is no harm done in periodically bringing up the importance of assessment, distributing articles to the team that show how other teams have evaluated themselves, even pressing the issue at periodic milestones.

12. **Q.** *What if a team member feels that the team is totally ineffective and not achieving its goals? What should he or she do?*

  A. The team member is making an assessment that may or may not be accurate. Obviously, there are strong feelings here that need to be addressed to the team as a whole. I encourage the member to write down specific team behaviors that are causing problems and then bring them to the team leader, facilitator, or the team as a whole. If everyone refuses to listen or address the concerns, I suggest that the member resign from the team and give his or her energies to a team that is moving ahead.

Notes

1. Jack Gordon, "The Team Troubles That Won't Go Away," *Training Magazine* (August 1994): 31.
2. Adapted from *Campbell-Hallam Team Development Survey* (Colorado Springs, Colo.: NCS Assessments).
3. J. Milliman, R. Zawacki, C. Norman, L. Powell, and J. Kirksey, "Companies Evaluate Employees From All Perspectives," *Personnel Journal* (November 1994): 99–102.
4. "Creating Teams in a Hurry—With Focus and Without Fear," *Total Quality* (August 1993): 4.

8

New Roles for Everybody—From Supervisors to Suppliers

The complaint was clear: The manager had been to training, participated in the role plays, and pondered the case studies, but when it came time to act as a coach for the cross-functional project team, he made mistake after mistake. He constantly canceled appointments with individual team members and often failed to attend team meetings; he handed off projects to the team and provided no direction or follow-through; he was unavailable and uncommunicative when the team tried to straighten out the problems. Was this a bad manager? No, just one who was greatly overextended and had little time to interact with a project team he had created. If necessary, he could be a coach, but for him, other needs usually took priority over the team's.

In the team environment, managers and supervisors are responsible for observing and working with teams to improve the level of communication, decision making, leadership, adherence to team norms, conflict management, and overall climate. The leadership must observe and diagnose the team's dynamics and develop a way of relating to the team that is different from the methods used in the past. As the team matures, the leader's role shifts from identifying the team's tasks and controlling decision making to emphasizing consultation, two-way communication, and joint decision making. A team of MIS managers described the managerial roles before teams in these terms:

180

- Leaders who focused responsibility on particular resources or functions
- Fixers and rectifiers
- Decision makers
- Interpreters of senior management's focus
- Motivators
- Conflict resolvers
- Guidance counselors
- Organizers and expediters

They felt their employees viewed them as:

- Evaluators
- Supervisors who were slow to react and respond and who were "separate" from the workers
- Ineffective
- Technicians
- All-knowing
- Responsible for filling all the voids, both personal and business
- People who were allowed no bad days

The managers realized the substantial amount of work required to change these perceptions in order to shift to a team environment. While they saw the problems, they also recognized that the perceptions would not be changed overnight.

Making the Shift to Teams

In many cases not enough attention is paid to the amount of stress the new culture is creating for managers and supervisors. They see their jobs as becoming obsolete and are uncertain about what the future will hold.[1] The following stress points affect their ability to function as coaches in the new environment:

Key Stress Points for Managers and Supervisors

- Changing roles from first-line supervisor to new roles such as facilitator/trainer

Q&A
#2

* Determining how to give the teams meaningful decision-making authority without risking poor results
* Juggling established policies and procedures with new ones
* Feeling responsible for early team mistakes
* Jumping in to fix things because of lack of prompt decision making by the team
* Determining how to refocus a team's mission when it's getting stale
* Defining a role for themselves that effectively utilizes their skills without undercutting the growth of teams

The plant manager of a wire company dropped in on his design team to see how things were going. He wanted to ask a few questions and check on the implementation of the cellular teams. As he started to interject his opinions, the facilitator interrupted to say that he wasn't on their planned agenda but that the team would be happy to include him under "other business." He was a good sport and complimented the team on its organization and spunk.

Q&A
#3

The role of managers and supervisors is changing. James Champy in his book *Re-Engineering Management* reports that 1.4 million executive, managerial, and administrative positions were eliminated between 1989 and 1994.[2] It's a frightening time for this level of people in many organizations, and they know it.

During the early implementation of self-directed teams in one manufacturing company, the plant manager was particularly difficult. Although he wanted the results that can be achieved

Q&A
#9

with teams, he had no patience for the process. Sometimes it was necessary to "get in his face" and tell him he had to change. To counteract and limit the impact of this individual, we created what we called a resource team whose purpose was obstensibly to oversee the implementation of teams in the organization. The hidden agenda was to control the plant manager. The resource team was so effective, not only for this organization but for others that have used it as well, that it has become a mainstay in our process of creating and maintaining teams. It was especially valuable in providing the extra support needed for managers and supervisors in transition.

The Resource Team

The resource team is composed of managers and supervisors who have direct contact with the team. They meet regularly to:

* Act as a steering committee to draft team charters
* Discuss the team's progress, assist in cutting red tape, and encourage evaluation
* Oversee the needs of external customers
* Ensure that customer expectations are met during implementation of teams
* Study the entire technical system and identify what needs to be redesigned
* Provide a network of management support; give presentations to other groups
* Look at how the present system works socially and evaluate ways that redesign could create greater job satisfaction and enrichment
* Examine all aspects of the current system—hiring, firing, training, planning, scheduling, compensating, and repairing—and look for opportunities to improve
* Visit companies already working in teams and report observations and ideas to internal teams
* Provide information to the teams on customer requirements, safety, quality, finance/business, goals, statistical process control (SPC), maintenance, vendors/suppliers, quantity, materials, machines, and costs
* Determine the methodology for technical and skills training; evaluate results
* Provide input on rate of team implementation
* Develop guidelines for the measurement of team activities and monitor cost effectiveness and progress
* Establish and deliver appropriate rewards and recognition
* Introduce self-direction, empowerment, and other team concepts throughout the organization
* Sustain the interaction and functional links with other interrelated and interdependent groups
* Identify and implement specific ways to praise and recog-

nize the contributions of the teams and encourage the celebration of success

Coaching as a Resource Team

When the resource team is reviewing the progress of specific teams, it is functioning as a coach. Here is a step-by-step process when one team is coaching another.

Functions of a Resource Team as Coach

1. Assess knowledge, skills, and abilities of the team. Examine the level of education, experience, and aptitude. Does the team have the tools to do the job?
2. Clarify the standards and expectations. Do the team members know what is important in terms of results?
3. Identify the help needed in terms of budget, equipment, and support from the resource team.
4. Measure the team's level of motivation and its willingness to do the task. Are the intrinsic and extrinsic rewards aligned with the team environment and sufficient to motivate?
5. Check the amount of day-to-day feedback and coaching with the team. Are the members receiving useful feedback on a regular basis? Who on the resource team is maintaining regular contact?
6. Determine whether the team is headed in the correct direction based on the policies of the organization.
7. Identify and assess the influences in the environment that are outside the team's control. How are negative influences being minimized?

Key Coaching Behaviors for a Resource Team

- Regular assessment of the teams in action
- Observation on a weekly basis
- Written reports based on assessment data
- Discussions with teams
- Monitoring of results
- Public discussions and meetings

* Sharing information and data
* Wandering around and talking with team members informally

Each member of a resource team was given five praise cards (see Figure 8-1) to distribute to any team that was doing a good job that week. Despite the fact that each resource team member had talked about the importance of recognizing good performance, only one person (on a team of twelve) had actually delivered the praise cards by the next meeting. In another plant forty miles away, the plant manager had the cards made up on notepads with the plant insignia for all the managers and supervisors to use. People are regularly handing out complimentary comments there, and positive results can be seen. Managers enjoy taking the minute or so to jot down a compliment and put it on a team member's work station. One member actually enlarged his note in the copier and hung it from the side of his computer.

As teams are launched throughout the organization, each member of the resource team becomes a team champion for one or more of the organizational teams. In the wire company, the resource team, which the company calls a design team, had been quite ineffective in implementing and overseeing the teams until each member was assigned the role of team champion. After that meeting, the members, half of whom are hourly employees, all held one-on-one sessions with the cellular teams and reported back at the next design team meeting. The whole tone and direction changed as members reported real-life situations that needed

Figure 8-1. Praise card.

Thanks for what you did: _____
_____
(specific and clear behavior)
As a result of your actions, _____
_____
(what they accomplished)
_____   _____
signature   date

their help. The design team has revised its team champion description to make certain that members don't intervene too early to fix the team's problems.

The Role of Team Champion

- Help the team stay focused on its mission, production goals, measurements, and boundaries, including assisting with the preparation and oversight of the team's budget.
- Help team members bring their knowledge and experience to bear on solving problems.
- Develop team's decision-making skills.
- Assist with the implementation of the team's decisions.
- Expand the team's range of effectiveness.
- Analyze the team's readiness for new tasks.
- Train the team to perform the tasks.
- Monitor and coach.
- Help remove barriers to performance.
- Locate the necessary tools, information, and resources to get the job done.
- Encourage innovation and measured risk taking.
- Share key information with the team on a daily basis.
- Make team members genuine business partners.
- Build shared ownership of activities and results.
- Help the team learn and grow from mistakes.
- Encourage continuous improvement of methods and processes.
- Build the commitment of the team to its own success and to the success of other teams and the whole organization.
- Inspire positive interactions.
- Help the team foresee and influence change and develop methods for adapting to it.
- Encourage and suggest continuous learning in interpersonal, administrative, and technical training areas.
- Help team members learn how to respect their differences, and build respect for diverse points of view.
- Rechannel nonproductive conflict within the team.
- Be a living example of values that promote teamwork.
- Function as a resource person to the team.

♦ Set the standards and help the team maintain them.
♦ Keep the team energized and moving forward.
♦ Help the team recognize what it's done well and how to learn from its mistakes.
♦ Guide the team to be responsive to market/customer information.
♦ Translate customer requests into practical business opportunities.
♦ Serve as a liaison between the resource team and the team itself.
♦ Forward team concerns for management discussion and resolution.
♦ Guide management in assessing the team's performance for compensation and performance evaluation decisions.

We have also found it effective for the resource team members to function as coaches or mentors to managers, supervisors, and professional staff who are just learning about teams. The accountability established in the mentor-learner relationship significantly improves training results (see Chapter 3).

In the team environment, managers, supervisors, and professional and technical staff have new sets of responsibilities for themselves as individuals as well. Their role is twofold: do tasks within the existing system and look for opportunities to challenge the existing system. A group of managers, supervisors, and professional staff in a training session developed its own job descriptions. As the group shared its results, members of the other groups were asked, "Is there anything else you want this group of people to do?" For the managers, the group responded, "Be honest and be supportive." Notice that commanding and controlling activities are not on the list.

┌─────┐
│ Q&A │
│ #4 │
└─────┘

Job Descriptions for Supervisors in Transition

Within the system:

♦ Share the vision—talk it up.
♦ Hand off tasks; explain, explain, explain.
♦ Evaluate capabilities and results.
♦ Define training needs.

- Motivate; give words of support.
- Recognize what is being done correctly now.
- Work side-by-side with the team for a short time.
- Gather and provide feedback for the team
- Assist with understanding customer expectations/needs.
- Provide individual recognition.
- Give guidance.

Challenging the system:

- Identify how to do things better.
- Identify tasks that can be eliminated.
- Provide group recognition.
- Encourage self-evaluation.
- Help the team explore different points of view.

Job Descriptions for Managers in Transition

Within the system:

- State the vision.
- Identify which tasks can be handed off.
- Assess skill levels.
- Identify training needs.
- Become more business-focused.
- Empower supervisors.
- Teach others.
- Find the necessary tools, information, and resources to help the team.
- Accept failure as a learning tool.
- Communicate; share information.
- Restate desired outcomes and boundaries as needed.
- Help the team define customer expectations.
- Forecast and plan for the future.

Challenging the system:

- Identify and remove barriers to change.
- Identify what we can do better.
- Determine if a task adds value to the organization.
- Figure out how to measure success.

• Automate and eliminate job tasks.
• Organize and structure work better.
• Benchmark with other organizations.
• Become involved with operators on a daily basis (less hiding behind doors).
• Encourage improved work processes and partnerships.

Job Descriptions for Professional/Technical Staff in Transition

Within the system:

• Share common goals.
• Keep information channels open.
• Promote involvement and feedback.
• Promote ownership and accountability.
• Set up progress measurements.
• Provide training.
• Give maximum support in the early stages of learning.
• Learn how to deal with resistance.
• Take risks.
• Interface between other groups.

Challenging the system:

• Ask more "what, where, how" questions.
• Share benefits.
• Stop working in a vacuum.
• Broaden work scope.
• Give more responsibility to the teams.
• Acknowledge diversity of thinking.
• Promote change.

The Job of Coach

A large portion of the new job responsibilities for managers and supervisors involves coaching. Coaching is a term that has become popular in recent years. Although the term is bandied about, few managers and supervisors are clear about what it means to be a coach.

The person most likely to be considered the team's coach is its former supervisor. The coach is responsible for creating an environment that allows the team to lead and the coach to remain on the sidelines while giving day-to-day feedback aimed at improving the team's performance. The coach's style needs to vary on the basis of the amount of direction the team needs, the amount of support needed, and the level of the team's involvement in decision making. The coaching process requires the person to place authority with a process that encourages the team to take increasing control.

Key Functions of the Coach

* Involves the team in problem identification; helps the team achieve agreement about what needs to change or be accomplished
* Helps the team discuss possible approaches to the task or alternative solutions to a problem
* Helps the team agree on specific action to be taken and the results expected
* Reviews the team's action plans to provide ideas, resources, and opinions if solicited
* Teaches technical, interpersonal, and support skills; fosters a learning environment by helping team members learn, grow, and develop
* Builds relationships by spending time with the team; offers guidance, support, and coaching
* Actively listens and facilitates problem solving
* Encourages risk taking and experimentation
* Delegates authority and responsibility
* Promotes shared information and collaborative problem solving
* Offers praise and recognition; recognizes accomplishments
* Monitors and assesses performance by observing and talking to the team members and others
* Provides formal and informal constructive feedback
* Connects the team to other groups and integrates their efforts with those of others
* Models behavior by showing an appreciation for diversity of thought, style, and behavior

An effective coach converts these responsibilities into a coaching action plan (see Figure 8-2) that includes specific ways to help the team set goals, train people, build relationships, motivate the teams, monitor performance, and provide feedback. Teams usually need coaching when:

* A team member expresses concern about a process
* A team member suggests that a process be done differently
* A customer makes a request for something special because of a safety concern and the team member is relaying the information to the coach
* A team member questions why a procedure is necessary
* A team member suggests combining several pieces of paperwork into a single form
* Two team members ask for the same vacation time off

As a self-directed work team began to take over the duties of its supervisor, management became more and more confused about its role. Some managers felt strongly that it was important to back off and let the team find its own way and make its own mistakes. Others felt the need to be more involved. The result was a mess of mixed messages that confused the team completely. At that point, management had to make a decision about its role.

When Should Management Coach and When Should It Direct?

When to coach:

* When the "how" or method of doing something doesn't matter a lot
* When the team knows how to do the task
* When the team has already done it before
* When the team did it right the last time
* When the team is deciding on process steps
* When it's important that the team experience the pain associated with struggle, growth, and behavior change
* When the team is emotionally ready

When to direct:

* When the decision involves legal or policy (safety) issues
* When the team doesn't know what to do

Figure 8-2. Coaching action plan.

1. *Help the team set goals:*
   - What goals do you have for your team?

   - What milestones do you have for the team along the way?

   - How are your goals being communicated? How often?

2. *Train people:*
   - What needs to be taught to them?

   - What is the best way to teach it?

   - When should the skills be taught?

3. *Build relationships:*
   - What specific things are you doing to build relationships?

   - How often do you do face-to-face coaching?

4. *Motivate the teams:*
   - What reward systems do you have in place?

   - Do the rewards make clear what behavior is being rewarded?

---

5. *Monitor performance:*
   • Is the team doing what it is supposed to be doing?

   • How often are you checking? What methods are you using?

   • How are you gradually increasing the team's responsibility?

---

6. *Provide feedback:*
   • How do you let them know how it is doing?

   • Are you maintaining a scoreboard that is meaningful for the team?

• When the team has never done the task before
• When the team did it wrong the last time
• When the "what" (experience, knowledge, information) is not apparent
• When one right way exists
• When the team is emotionally insecure

A coach cannot influence a team's behavior from a distance. An uninvolved coach won't have the information needed and won't know the team's concerns, and the distance between the coach and the team will lead the team to view the coach as an adversary.

Characteristics of a Good Coach

• Is interested in people
• Is predictable
• Is straightforward
• Lets people know where they stand

+ Gives credit to others
+ Builds confidence
+ Has high standards
+ Is objective
+ Is firm but fair
+ Is a good teacher
+ Makes the team want to do their best
+ Understands the processes and procedures

So much of a supervisor's ability to function in the new team environment derives from attitude. All supervisors go through a period of time when they are unclear about the future of their jobs—both whether a job will exist and, if it does exist, what will it be. The ones who have made the transition best have been open to change, willing to live with temporary ambiguity about their jobs, and eager to experiment with the role of a coach. They have exhibited these behaviors:

+ Ask for help.
+ Take criticism without being defensive.
+ Provide constructive feedback.
+ Support coworkers.
+ Share control by giving up leadership periodically.
+ Compliment other people's work.
+ Share information.
+ Facilitate a discussion.
+ Verbally support other workers' suggestions.
+ Share feelings with others.
+ Deal directly with a conflict situation.
+ Share control.
+ Act on feedback from someone else.
+ Listen without interruption.
+ Ask questions before giving personal opinion.
+ Ask for suggestions from others.
+ Provide guidance when the team is stuck or floundering.
+ Support the team's authority and decisions.

Mistakes Coaches Make

+ Trying to coach at a distance
+ Not gathering enough information or analyzing the situation before making a coaching intervention

- Not knowing the team's concerns
- Coaching only when there is a problem
- Lecturing instead of coaching
- Dealing in generalities and making assumptions
- Not anticipating the reaction of the team to certain situations
- Giving evaluative, controlling feedback
- Making assumptions about why something happened or why people did what they did
- Jumping in too quickly with a coaching invention

The most important function for many coaches is to give effective feedback that will guide and influence behavior. A good coach corrects behavior and leaves self-esteem intact.

Effective Coaching Feedback

- Is *descriptive in nature*—"We're having trouble getting the correct information to the customer."
- Is *problem-oriented*—"What could the team do to reduce the number of mistakes?"
- Is *empathetic*—"If I understand what you feel, you're unhappy that you have to be team leader again."
- Is *empowering*—"I think it's your responsibility to suggest some options."
- Is *exploring*—"I really do want to know what you think of the idea."

Ineffective Coaching Feedback

- Is *negatively projecting*—"This team is never going to get anywhere if you don't learn to. . . ."
- Is *close-minded*—"We can discuss it but the bottom line will be my way."
- Is *authoritative*—"We originally planned to do it this way, and we are going to do it this way."
- Is *purposefully confusing*—"I would say we should not be unhappy."
- Is *judgmental and demoralizing*—"Don't ever tell me that

you're doing your best, because I can always find someone
who'll do it better."
* Is *deceptive*—"My mind is always open as you know, but
I'm not going to approve it."

Although organizations expect employees to have difficulty
working in teams, in most cases it is managers and supervisors
who have the more difficult transition. They fear loss in status as
it becomes obvious that there is little use for the old roles and
practices. One supervisor, after watching the excellent video
Everybody Leads, which details the history of the self-directed
teams at the Rohm-Hass chemical plant in Kentucky, said, "What
happens to us if we don't want to be a facilitator or trainer? That
one guy didn't look too happy to me."

Personal Coping Strategies for Coaches

The transition from the role of traditional supervisor or manager
to the role of coach, advisor, mentor, and facilitator causes considerable stress for most people. Here are some coping strategies to
help with the stress:

1. Acknowledge that the stress exists; take part in a stress
   reduction class where relaxation techniques are taught.
2. Use basic time management techniques to help with the
   increased demand on time.
3. Share concerns and confusion with colleagues and/or a
   mentor who will listen and help you sort through the feelings and concerns.
4. Hold off judging whether the change will be successful
   or not.
5. List the possible benefits of your new role; think positively
   about the transition.
6. Be a part of the resource team responsible for implementation.

JOSTENS' Princeton, Illinois, jewelry plant has been using
self-directed cellular teams for a number of years with excellent
results. The plant manager attributes some of the success to the

matrix organizational chart the company designed, which puts former supervisors in charge of eight specific areas of coordination (Chapter 2 details the team responsibilities) and calls them team development leaders.

Eight Sample Team Development Leader Roles

1. *Administrative leadership coordinator*—oversees budget development, adherence to policies and procedures, paperwork, peer reviews, decision-making skills
2. *Quality leadership coordinator*—oversees quality standards, measurements, adherence to standards, customer requirements
3. *Production leadership coordinator*—oversees production quotas, safety, and workflow
4. *Processes leadership coordinator*—oversees design requirements, process improvement, and equipment
5. *Training leadership coordinator*—oversees technical and team skill development, new employee selection
6. *Supplies and materials leadership coordinator*—oversees supplier relations, criteria and standards, inventory
7. *Work environment leadership coordinator*—oversees team cohesiveness, conflicts, culture, safety, maintenance
8. *Customer relations/tours leadership coordinator*—oversees external and internal customer focus, communication

General Functions of a Team Development Leader

- Coordinate leadership for all leadership roles on teams plant wide
- Work and assist with transition of team leadership responsibilities for assigned teams
- Work and assist teams with trouble shooting and problem solving for assigned teams
- Work and assist team as needed to gain support from other areas for assigned teams
- Contact person for technical customer service questions about products and processes
- Coordinate special requests and custom designs from customer service and design area

- Coordinate new product development
- Oversee assigned security functions

New Roles for Teams

Managers and supervisors are not the only ones wearing new hats. Many roles on the teams are changing as job sharing becomes a given. The most common new roles for teams involve the handling of administrative tasks and doing problem-solving and project-planning tasks. However, as the team advances into the middle years, its role can be expanded to include some typical human resources functions, such as hiring and training.

Using Teams to Hire New People

For several years a small business had been using staff informally during its hiring process to get employees' impressions about applicants for various positions. As the organization moved toward the use of teams, it decided to formalize the process by creating formal hiring teams. Here's what it did:

1. Created a cross-functional hiring team composed of managerial and hourly staff, both inside and outside the functional area of the open position.
2. Trained the hiring team in interviewing skills, meeting the requirements of the Americans with Disabilities Act (ADA) and other legal stipulations, and group decision making.
3. Paired members to form interview subteams responsible for specific areas of questioning. The members created the questions and rehearsed their interviews in advance. Of particular importance was learning how to probe beyond the initial response to a question and identifying discrepancies in what the applicant was saying.
4. Had each team develop a set of criteria (see Figure 8-3) for selecting the ideal applicant, place the criteria on a grid, and review and score the resumes on the grid to identify the top applicants for interviewing.
5. Used team members for other jobs as well, with team

(Text continues on page 202.)

Figure 8–3a. Chart for screening applications.

Decision Criteria

Candidate Name	Comments	Familiarity with TQM	Prof. training experience	Development of materials	Team training	Communications training	SPC training	Quality or training sample	Degree of initiative	Decision making	Managerial skills	Team experience	Count

(continues)

Figure 8-3a. (cont.)

Candidate Name	Comments	SDWT experience	Management of priorities	Manufacturing experience	HR background	Measurement systems	Gov't. regulations—health & safety	Budgeting	Quality of written materials	College degree	Computer skills	Count

Decision Criteria

Figure 8-3b. Criteria descriptions for chart for screening applications.

Using the chart for screening applications, rank each candidate on a scale from 1 to 5 for each area. The key below will give you assistance in determining the score:

Familiarity with TQM philosophy/values
    1: Exposure to
    5: Uses on daily basis
Professional training experience with all levels of staff
    1: Not clear whether conducts training
    5: Meets five-year minimum and regularly conducts training
Development of training materials (depth)
    1: Not clear
    5: Exceeds three-year minimum
Specific training experience in team-related topics
    1: Not apparent
    5: Has trained in various topics
Specific training experience in communication skills
    1: Not apparent
    5: Has trained in various topics
Specific training experience in statistical process control
    1: Not apparent
    2: Has trained in various topics
Quality of training sample
    1: Outline vague/incomplete
    5: Fully developed program
Degree of initiative/level of autonomy
    1: Not clear
    5: Show initiative/autonomy in projects
Decision-making authority
    1: Low level
    5: High level
Managerial skills
    1: Not clear/lack of
    5: Job experience is described as using these skills
Experience with organizational and cross-functional teams
    1: Exposure to
    5: Uses on a daily basis

(continues)

Figure 8-3b. (cont.)

Experience with self-directed work teams
   1: Exposure to
   5: Uses on a daily basis
Experience with managing multiple priorities/projects
   1: Very limited job duties
   5: Variety in duties mentioned in positions
Manufacturing direct experience/background
   1: Low
   5: Five years +
Human Resources background
   1: Low
   5: Five years +
Direct experience with measurement systems
   1: No
   5: Yes
Familiarity with government regulations—health and safety
   1: No
   5: Yes
Budgeting experience
   1: No
   5: Yes
Experience in developing written materials/resume/cover letter/
training sample presentation
   1: Poor quality
   5: Excellent quality
College degree or equivalent
   1: No
   5: Yes
Computer skills
   1: Weak (word processing only)
   3: Moderate (word processing plus spreadsheet)
   5: Excellent (word processing, dbase, spreadsheet, etc.)

members assigning themselves these responsibilities: recordkeeper, who was responsible for maintaining all the formal records of the applicants for the team; the contact person, who made travel and overnight accommodations and maintained contact with each of the applicants throughout the process; and the host, who greeted the applicants at the business site and escorted them to the various interview locations.

Figure 8-4. Team summary sheet.

Team Summary Sheet

Candidate _____

Position _____

Date _____

Job Requirements:

Direct impression *(all complete)*	5	4	3	2	1	0
Job knowledge & skills	5	4	3	2	1	0
Teambuilding & delegation	5	4	3	2	1	0
Planning & forecasting	5	4	3	2	1	0
Interpersonal skills & conflict resolution	5	4	3	2	1	0

Total Score _____

Special Notations:

Recommendation:

_____ Hire _____ Reject
_____ Refer for _____ position

---

6. Had each interview pair rate each applicant after the interview for the team's specific area, as well as for overall impression. Scoring sheets were sent to the recordkeeper, who compiled scores for each of the applicants (see Figures 8-4 and 8-5).

7. Developed realistic role plays to conduct with applicants

(Text continues on page 206.)

Figure 8-5. Team interviewer's report.

Applicant	Position

Date	Interviewer

Directions: Write your analysis and interpretation of interview information for each section. Summarize the candidate's strengths and shortcomings and write your summary and recommendations. Then circle an appropriate rating for each section based on your evaluation (5=excellent; 4=better than average; 3=fully qualified; 2=less than fully qualified; 1=unacceptable; 0=not observed). Compare results with your interview partner and complete a fresh form that combines both sets of notes and averages the scoring. Turn this form in to the designated person at the end of the day.

DIRECT IMPRESSION (Impact)	Appearence Manner Self-expression Responsiveness
5 4 3 2 1 0	
JOB KNOWLEDGE & SKILLS	
5 4 3 2 1 0	
TEAM BUILDING & DELEGATION	
5 4 3 2 1 0	

PLANNING & FORECASTING 5 4 3 2 1 0	
INTERPERSONAL SKILLS & CONFLICT RESOLUTION 5 4 3 2 1 0	

SUMMARY OF STRENGTHS **(+)**	**SUMMARY OF SHORTCOMINGS** **(–)**	

OVERALL SUMMARY AND RECOMMENDATIONS

1. In favor of hiring (stress value and assets)

2. Against hiring (stress risks or liabilities)

3. Final recommendations (gauge strength of candidate; consider placement, supervision, training, and potential)

to determine how the applicants would respond in particular situations. Often these provided the team with helpful insights that could not be gleaned from the more formal, staged interviews.

8. Had each team decide who to keep and who to eliminate, based on the initial criteria for selection, including minimal composite scores allowed.

Another option developed by the team was a lunchtime interview with what was called the informal hiring team—a voluntary group of employees who were interested in the candidates and wanted to ask questions.

Considerations in Planning the Team Hiring Process

1. Who should receive the applications for positions in our area?
2. Who should do the preliminary screening?
3. Who should interview top candidates?
4. Who decides who should be offered the position?
5. Who is responsible for notifying those not selected?
6. How will each team member be involved?
7. What training is required?

Division of Tasks and Responsibilities on a Hiring Team

1. *Host tasks/responsibilities*
   - Develop interview schedule for hiring team members.
   - Develop interview schedule for candidates; mail schedule with cover letter to applicant.
   - Coordinate use of offices during on-site interviews.
   - Check that offices have been set up properly for the interview.
   - Coordinate lunch arrangements.
   - Function as a "stringer" throughout the interview schedule.
   - Provide refreshments and directions, and see to personal needs.
2. *Interview Coordinator Task Responsibilities*
   - Oversee the development of any testing materials.

- Oversee the development of interviewing questions.
- Review all questions from the subteams to avoid duplication.
- Send corrections/suggestions back to interview pairs for consideration.
- Distribute master set of all interview questions to interview teams prior to visit.

3. *Candidate Contact Task/Responsibilities*
   - Contact candidates prior to interview to express welcome.
   - Coordinate with candidate for pickup.
   - Make meal and lodging reservations (if needed).
   - Administer written tests during on-site interview.
   - Discuss any questions still unaddressed at the end of the interview session.
   - Follow up with candidate to keep individual posted about the status of the interviewing process.

4. *Recordkeeper Task/Responsibilities*
   - Keep master records of all applicant information.
   - Keep a master set of all interview questions (oral and written).
   - Distribute applicant scoring forms to team members; summarize and compile returned forms for review by interview team.
   - Keep a master set of all related correspondence.
   - Send rejection letter as appropriate.

Using Team Members for Behavioral Role Plays in Hiring

Using sample scenarios appropriate to the workplace, team members can role-play situations, asking the applicant to participate by responding as he or she naturally would. A third member of the team acts as the observer and takes notes on how the applicant responded.

Sample Role-Play Situations

- "A member of the quality team is continually critical of the team approach to management. She frequently makes sarcastic and negative comments during team meetings and outside meetings to other employees. The two of you are sitting together in the break room when she says, 'You would have really loved it here before all this team stuff started.' Please respond." At this point the team member repeats the statement said and the role play begins. (The team is measuring the applicant's open-mindedness, ability to ask questions for better understanding, ability to state her own viewpoint, and ability to engage another person in conversation.)

♦ "The production and art departments have worked independently since their inception. Now you want to enhance their combined operation. You've called the two departments together for their first joint meeting under your direction. Proceed with your introduction." (The team is looking for how the applicant introduces change and evaluating his ability to draw people out and to deal with resistance.)

♦ "You had twenty-four hours to meet a deadline on a project, and there was no way you could get your team together for a final decision. You made the decision alone in order to meet the deadline. Now a staff member is confronting you, saying, 'This isn't the way we do things here! We decide by consensus!' Please respond." (The team is checking for backbone and ability to explain, listen, and bring employee to a point of understanding.)

Benefits of Hiring Teams

* Substantial increase in existing employees' enthusiasm and commitment toward a new employee
* Development of interviewing (questioning) skills that can be transferred to many other tasks (e.g., handling customers)
* Growth in ability to make decisions based on data and impressions
* Values clarification among various levels of staff in an organization
* New relationships between people who may not frequently have an opportunity to work together

Using Teams as In-House Trainers

As the team process expands throughout organizations, many companies find they cannot afford to hire outside consultants and trainers for all the training. Creating an in-house training team can help to refresh some members who enjoy the change in routine and the new skill development.

Selection Criteria for In-House Trainers

+ Choose people who not only enjoy teaching and relating to others but also have a zest for learning. When a person has only memorized a script, it's easy to poke holes in the information he presents. In-house trainers must constantly increase their background knowledge and their ability to apply the learning in the workplace.

+ If the individual is doing other tasks besides training, give training a high priority. Many supervisors who are trying to balance numerous job responsibilities go into their training session ill-prepared and harried. Do not select someone who is already overloaded.

+ Test presentation skills by asking the would-be trainer to introduce herself and to divide a hypothetical team into a group activity. Listen for enthusiasm, vocal tone, eye contact. Imagine the impact this person would have talking with you for three hours. Could she sustain your interest?

+ Encourage the in-house trainer to participate in the module first before training it. Watch to see how he acts as a participant.

+ Select individuals with poise and maturity and who are slow to anger.

+ Set high standards for the trainer's behavior (e.g., punctuality, preparation, good grooming).

Launching the In-House Trainers

+ All trainers should be trained in adult learning theory so that they understand why training is presented in specific ways.

• Create a team of trainers whenever possible so that the trainers can help and encourage each other.
• Use an experienced professional trainer to help the in-house trainers with techniques, delivery, and content.
• Teach specific skills (e.g., effective ways to work in small groups, how to use flipcharts and overhead projectors, how to introduce exercises and videos).
• Require "dry runs" to see exactly what the training will look like before the actual session. If the trainers are not ready, do not use them in the session.
• Hire an outside trainer to sit in on sessions periodically and assess the training quality.

Common Mistakes With In-House Training

• Creating high expectations for the amount of training in-house trainers (e.g., former supervisors) can do
• Believing training is easy after watching professional trainers
• Failing to recognize the need for or to allow time for preparation and reading
• Not using in-house trainers to develop real-life examples, role plays, and case studies
• Inflating feedback or being too gentle with negative feedback in an attempt to encourage trainers without providing accurate feedback on their performance

External Relationships

The new organization has changed both the roles within its walls and its external relationships with customers and suppliers. The team process requires new relationships not only with managers, supervisors, and technical staff but with customers and suppliers as well. These days it's likely that a production team member, a team member from customer service, an engineer, and the production facilitator/supervisor might all get together to work through a customer problem. The more familiar these people are with the needs of the customer, the more quickly they will be able to satisfy those needs.

Learning About the Customer

+ Create a subteam to identify all customers. Find out everything about them and report back to the team.
+ Invite customers to attend team meetings and have face-to-face meetings with team members. Ask them to explain how they use the product or service, what they like or dislike about it, and improvements they would like you to make. Listen for customer expectations.
+ Share information about the team (history, charter, development process, quality measures) and what it can provide. Work to establish a relationship with the customer.
+ Solicit customer feedback on a regular basis, and use the feedback continuously to improve the team's work.

Tips for Talking With Customers

+ Work in pairs to help gather information and share insights.
+ Ask "how, what, when, where" questions.
+ Probe for the specifics behind any generalized statements.
+ Respond to negative feedback by noting that you understand the problem and desire to make it right.
+ Restate and paraphrase to make certain you understood the customer's key points.
+ Avoid making promises that the team cannot deliver.
+ Follow up with the customer on any action the team takes as a result of the customer's feedback.

If the customer is the one who receives the product or service, then the supplier is the one who provides the people, materials, equipment, information, procedures, time, and money to create that product or service. Quality organizations recognize that this is one continuous chain, with each part dependent on the other. As teams grow in confidence and ability, it makes sense for them also to work on the supplier relationship.

Learning About the Supplier

* Identify the team suppliers, both external and internal.
* Define what you expect of each supplier (products, services).
* Meet with the supplier and communicate the team's overall objectives and performance requirements.
* Give the suppliers time to speak about their needs, wants, and desires, how they approach things, and their limitations.
* Write down all the agreements reached between the team and the supplier.
* Set up a regular feedback and follow-up schedule.
* Monitor supplier performance using observation, data gathering, team satisfaction ratings, and periodic visits to the supplier's site.
* Give feedback to the supplier on a continuous basis.

Development of a Cooperation Team

A joint cooperation team comprises representatives of both the organization and the supplier. Typically, it is led by the supplier's manager and includes team members from quality, manufacturing, engineering, customer service, and other functions. The task of the team is to identify improvements, resolve problems, and implement solutions. The team is responsible for opening and maintaining a line of communication between the company and the employees of the supplier who develop, produce, package, or service the product or service.

Team activities typically include:

* Mapping the supplier process
* Identifying process steps
* Eliminating unnecessary steps
* Reducing product/service cost

A team-based steering column manufacturer expanded its relationship with suppliers one step further. It asked suppliers to rate it as a customer. Then the team put on a banquet for the suppliers and shared the feedback it had received from them.

QUESTIONS AND ANSWERS:
New Roles for Everybody—From Supervisors to Suppliers

1. **Q.** *Isn't all this new role stuff just creating chaos for people?*

    A. In some ways you're right. Employees who used to just have to be concerned with their own jobs now are accountable for the work of their entire teams. Managers and supervisors now have to teach employees how to plan, organize, and control their work on teams instead of doing it themselves. It is definitely a new age in organizational development.

2. **Q.** *Is this change to the role of coach something that managers and supervisors are expected to do overnight?*

    A. Oh, no. It would be impossible to change that quickly. In fact, the transition usually takes one to two years. Under the best circumstances, the manager and supervisor gradually hand off responsibilities and accountability as the team matures and shows it is ready to handle them.

3. **Q.** *What are some of the new concepts that managers and supervisors have to understand in order to be able to handle the change?*

    A. Rollin Glaser[3] has identified six areas of learning for people who participate in teams: learning to cope with change; learning to accept responsibility for the team's work in addition to the supervisor's own work; learning group dynamics skills; learning to help the team to make the transition to increasing levels of empowerment; learning to think critically about work policies and processes; and learning to be a self-directed learner.

    He has also identified six areas of learning for the coach: learning a new leadership orientation; learning to empower people; learning to facilitate team self-management behaviors; learning personal coping strategies; learning to facilitate the learning of others; and learning to learn from experience.

Donna Deeprose in her book, *The Team Coach*, speaks specifically to the managers' role in coaching a team to self-manage its work and its members. "Your job will be a subtle one—to support the process, help keep it on track, ensure that all views are heard, encourage consensus, but discourage groupthink—all without appearing to step in and take over."[4]

4. **Q.** *I don't really see the benefits for me of changing to this new role. I really liked being a supervisor before, but now it's too demanding. Why should I like this change?*

    A. It's typically hard for supervisors to see the benefits in the beginning, so give yourself time. What other supervisors have identified as benefits include: the challenge and the mind-stretching experience, the new relationships formed, the freedom from routine work, the opportunity to watch other people grow in their abilities, and the chance to help people have better relationships. But some supervisors really like being supervisors and have difficulty with any new roles, regardless of how sweet management tries to make them.

5. **Q.** *We feel ashamed if we ask our old supervisor for help. What can we do?*

    A. There's nothing to be ashamed about, and, most likely, your supervisor will welcome the request. Most experts see the role of supervisor in the future as serving as a human relations expert and an external representative to other teams and levels of management. If you need help, it seems logical that your former supervisor is the person to ask.

6. **Q.** *What do you do with the specialist (e.g., engineer, accountant, technical writer, or electrician) who doesn't want to be a team player?*

    A. There's a place in the workforce for people who don't want to work in teams. It's important that we not act as if we all were made by cookie cutters. It may take some creative thinking to identify an effective place for this person, but I would definitely encourage you to do so.

7. **Q.** *Could you give me some specific behaviors that coaches are expected to do in the team environment—some real, down-to-earth examples?*

A. The coach's job might include the following: going over an activity and helping the team think it through before actually performing it; communicating the team's point of view to upper management; helping the team obtain equipment and supplies; encouraging open communication among team members who are learning new jobs; physically working with the group to help it do its work.

9. **Q.** *If you were to list the top five things organizations should do to create a supportive environment for teams, what would they be?*

A. First, organizations need to have a vision that is clear and engaging for the teams, managers, and supervisors. Next, the structure of the organization must foster competent performance, rewards, and continuous learning. The organization must provide training and support as teams mature and make sure that material resources are adequate and available. Finally, the organization needs to support its people as they experiment in this new and exciting age.

10. **Q.** *When you have a hiring team, what is the role of human resources?*

A. Human resources people are the subject matter experts (SMEs) who are heavily involved in the entire team hiring process. They conduct the initial hiring skills training and certify that the team is competent to do the interviewing and hiring without risk to the organization. Human resources monitors the actual interviews to make certain that team members are prepared and handle the interviews effectively. HR gives feedback to interviews, for example, if they do not probe deeply enough into what an applicant is saying. HR checks the written materials that become part of the applicant's file to be certain everything is in order. HR assists with any accommodations that are needed for the disabled. HR also handles the negotiation of salary and benefits with a candidate after the team has made its final selection. The list goes on and on. Suffice it to say that human resources is vital to the process.

11. **Q.** *Can you use the hiring team idea for internal hiring as well?*

A. Yes, though the team will need to be cautioned about discussing any information about the applicants outside the hiring team meetings. The selection process is also more difficult, especially if the team doesn't want to hire the internal applicant. Here's another spot where human resources can be a tremendous help to the team—processing feelings of guilt and deciding how to respond to the person after he doesn't get the job.

Notes

1. "Is Your Team Stressed?" *Quality Digest* (October 1994): 10.
2. James Campy, *Re-engineering Management* (New York: Harper-Collins, 1995), p. 19.
3. Rollin Glaser, "Helping Your Organization Gear Up for Self-Managing Teams," *Classic Readings in Self-Managing Teamwork* (King of Prussia, Pa.: Organization Design and Development, 1992), pp. 374–399.
4. Donna Deeprose, *The Team Coach* (New York: AMACOM, 1995).

Bibliography

Alexander, C. Phillip. "Voluntary Participation." *Quality Digest* (October 1994): 50–52.

Barker, Joel. *The Implications Wheel*. Minneapolis, Minn.: Aurora Pictures, 1994.

Berry, D., Cadwell, C., and Fehrmann, J. *50 Activities for Empowerment*. Mohegan Lake, N.Y.: MW Corporation, 1994.

Blake, Christopher. *Learning to Love*. Siloam Springs, Ark.: Concerned Communications, 1992.

Blake, R. R., Mouton, J. S., and McCause, A. A. *Organization by Design*. Reading, Mass.: Addison-Wesley, 1989.

Bledsoe, John. "Your Four Communicating Styles." *Training, The Magazine of Human Resources Development* (March 1976).

Block, P. *Stewardship*. San Francisco: Berrett-Kochler Publishers, 1993.

Blumberg, M. "Job Switching in Autonomous Work Groups." *Classic Readings in Self-Managing Teamwork*. King of Prussia, Pa.: Organization Design and Development, 1992.

Brassard, M., and Ritter, D. *The Memory Jogger*. Methuen, Mass.: GOAL/ OPC, 1994.

Brookes, Donald. "Designing Quality Compensation Systems." *Quality Digest* (April 1995).

Byham, W. C. *Zapp! The Lightning of Empowerment*. New York: Harmony Books, 1990.

Campbell, David, and Hallam, Glenn. *Campbell-Hallam Team Development Survey*. Colorado Springs, Colo.: Center for Creative Leadership, 1994.

Canetti, Elias. *Crowds and Power*. New York: Continuum Publishing, 1973.

Champy, James. *Reengineering Management*. New York: HarperCollins, 1995.

"Creating Teams in a Hurry—With Focus and Without Fear." *Total Quality* (August 1993): 4.

Courtright, John A. "A Laboratory Investigation of Groupthink." *Communication Monographs* 45 (1978).

Covey, Stephen. *Seven Habits of Highly Effective People.* New York: Simon and Schuster, 1989.

Crosby, R. *Walking the Empowerment Tightrope.* King of Prussia, Pa.: Organizational Design and Development, 1992.

Deeprose, Donna. *The Team Coach.* New York: AMACOM, 1995.

Deutsch, M. *The Resolution of Conflict.* New Haven: Yale University Press, 1973.

Dusharme, Dirk. "Is Your Team Stressed?" *Quality Digest* (October 1994): 10.

Fisher, K., Rayner, S., and Belgard, W. *Tips for Teams: A Ready Reference for Solving Common Team Problems.* New York: McGraw-Hill, 1995.

Gibb, Jack. *Trust: A New Vision of Human Relationships for Business, Education, Family and Personal Living.* North Hollywood, Calif.: Newcastle Publishing, 1991.

Glaser, Rollin. "Helping Your Organization Gear Up for Self-Managing Teams." *Classic Readings in Self-Managing Teamwork.* King of Prussia, Pa.: Organization Design and Development, 1992.

Goldher-Lerner, H. *Dance of Anger.* New York: Harper & Row, 1985.

Goodman, Paul A., and Associates. *Designing Effective Work Groups.* San Francisco: Jossey-Bass, 1986.

Gordon, Jack. "The Team Troubles That Won't Go Away." *Training Magazine* (August 1994): 31.

Gray, John. *Men Are From Mars, Women Are From Venus.* New York: HarperCollins, 1992.

Gross, Steven E. *Compensation for Teams.* New York: AMACOM, 1995.

Guzzo, R., Salas, E., and Associates. *Team Effectiveness and Decision-Making in Organizations.* San Francisco: Jossey-Bass, 1995.

Hackman, J. R. *Groups That Work (and Those That Don't): Creating Conditions for Effective Teamwork.* San Francisco: Jossey-Bass, 1990.

Hammer, Michael, and Champy, James. *Reengineering the Corporation.* New York: Harper Business, 1993.

Harbour, J. *The Process Reengineering Workbook.* New York: Quality Resources, 1994.

Harrington-Mackin, Deborah. *The Team Building Tool Kit.* New York: AMACOM, 1994.

Harper, A., and Harper, B. *Team Barriers: Actions for Overcoming the Barriers to Empowerment.* Mohegan Lake, N.Y.: MW Corporation, 1994.

Harvey, Jerry B. *The Abilene Paradox and Other Meditations on Management.* Lexington, Mass.: Lexington Books, 1988.

Harvey, Jerry. *Group Tyranny and the Gunsmoke Phenomenon.* Carlsbad, Calif.: CRM Films, 1991.

Hirschhorn, Larry. *Managing in the New Team Environment.* Reading, Mass.: Addison-Wesley, 1991.

Hitchcock, Darcy. "Getting Past the Top 10 Barriers to Successful Self-Directed Teams." *Total Quality* (September 1993): 4–5.

Holpp, Lawrence. "Applied Empowerment." *Training* (February 1994): 39–44.

Janis, I. "Groupthink." *Psychology Today* (November 1971): 43–46, 74–76.

———. *Victims of Groupthink.* Boston: Houghton-Mifflin, 1972.

Katzenbach, J. R., and Smith, D. K. *The Wisdom of Teams: Creating the High Performance Organization.* Boston: Harvard Business School, 1993.

Kelly, P. Keith. *Team Decision-Making Techniques.* Irvine, Calif.: Richard Chang & Associates, 1994.

Knowles, Malcolm and Hulda. *Introduction to Group Dynamics.* New York: Association Press, 1972.

Kroeger, Otto. *Type Talk at Work.* New York: Delacorte Press, 1992.

Landry, Tom, and G. Lewis. *Tom Landry: An Autobiography.* New York: Walker, 1991.

Lawler, E. E. III. *Strategic Pay: Aligning Organizational Strategies and Pay Systems.* San Francisco: Jossey-Bass, 1990.

Lawler, E. E. III, and Cohen, S. G. "Designing Pay Systems for Teams." *ACA Journal* (Autumn 1992): 6–17.

Lawler, E. E. III, Mohrman, Susan Albers, and Ledford, Gerald. *Employee Involvement and Total Quality Management: Practices and Results in Fortune 1000 Companies.* San Francisco: Jossey-Bass, 1992.

Lewis, Harriet R. T. *Crisis Pregnancy Center Volunteer Training Manual.* Falls Church, Va.: Christian Action Council, 1992.

Likert, R., and Likert, J. *New Ways of Managing Conflict.* New York: McGraw-Hill, 1976.

Luft, J. *Group Processes: An Introduction to Group Dynamics,* 3rd ed. Palo Alto, Calif.: Mayfield, 1984.

Maurer, Rick. "A Pillar of Strength." *TQM Magazine* (September/October, 1993).

Milliman, J., Zawacki, R., Norman, C. Powell, L., and Kirksey, J. "Companies Evaluate Employees From All Perspectives." *Personnel Journal* (November 1994): 99–102.

Mills, Daniel Quinn. *The Empowerment Imperative.* Amherst, Mass.: HRD Press, 1994.

Montemayor, Edilberto. "A Model for Aligning Teamwork and Pay." *ACA Journal* (1994).

Moravec, Milan, Juliff, Ron, and Hesler, Kathleen. "Partnerships Help a Company Manage Performance." *Personnel Journal* (January 1995): 104–108.

O'Neill, D., and Lough, D. "Team Incentives and TQM." *ACA Journal* (1994).

Orsburn, Jack, Moran, Linda, Musselwhite, Ed, and Zenger, John. *Self-Directed Work Teams: The New American Challenge.* Burr Ridge, Ill.: Irwin Professional Publishing, 1990.

Parker, G., and Kropp, R. *50 Activities for Self-Directed Teams.* Amherst, Mass.: HRD Press, 1994.

Peck, M. Scott. *The Different Drum: Community Making and Peace.* New York: Simon and Schuster, 1987.

Robbins, Harvey. *Turf Wars—Moving From Competition to Collaboration.* Midvale, Utah: Northwest Publishing, 1992.

Russo, E., and Eckler, Matthew. *Mastering Conflict.* King of Prussia, Pa.: Organizational Design and Development, 1995.

Schuster, Jay R., and Zingheim, Patricia K. "Building Pay Environments to Facilitate High Performance Teams." *ACA Journal* (Spring/Summer 1993): 40–51.

Senge, Peter M. *The Fifth Discipline.* New York: Doubleday/Currency, 1990.

Senge, Peter, M., Ross, B. Smith, Roberts, C., and Kleiner, A. *The Fifth Discipline Fieldbook.* Doubleday, New York. 1994.

Smitley, Williams, and Scott, David. "Empowerment: Unlocking the Potential of Your Work Force." *Quality Digest* (August 1994): 40–46.

"Supplier Scoring Keeps Quality Afloat." *Quality Digest* (News Digest section) (November 1994): 11.

"Team Tidbits." *Quality Progress* 28, no. 6 (June 1995): 18.

Thompson, Bradlee. "Negotiation Training: Win or What?" *Training Magazine* (June 1991): 33–34.

Total Quality Newsletter 5, no. 1 (Lakewood Publications, January 1994).

Total Quality Newsletter 4, no. 5, "Are Teams Worth It?" (Lakewood Publications, May 1993): 8.

Tuckman, B. W. "Development Sequences in Small Groups." *Psychological Bulletin* 63 (1965): 384–399.

Urey, William, and Fisher, Roger. *Getting to Yes: Negotiating Agreement Without Giving In.* New York: Penguin Books, 1983.

Vogt, J., and K., Murrell. *Empowerment in Organizations: How to Spark Exceptional Performance.* San Diego: Pfeiffer, 1990.

Weisbord, Marvin R. *Productive Workplaces.* San Francisco: Jossey-Bass, 1989.

Wheatley, Margaret. *Leadership and the New Science.* San Francisco: Berrett-Koehler Publisher, 1994.

Wheelwright, Joseph B. *Psychological Types*. San Francisco: C. G. Jung Institute of San Francisco, 1973.

Wilson, Jeanne, George, Jill, Wellins, Richard S., and Byham, William C. *Leadership Trapeze: Strategies for Leadership in Team-Based Organizations*. San Francisco: Jossey-Bass, 1994.

Zander, A. *Making Groups Effective*. San Francisco: Jossey-Bass, 1982.

Zenger, J., Musselwhite, E., Hurson, K., and Perrin, C. *Leading Teams: Mastering the New Role*. Homewood, Ill.: Irwin, 1994.

Zoglio, Suzanne. "Team Conflict Can Be a Constructive Force When It's Properly Managed." *Total Quality* (December 1994): 7.

Index

Abilene Paradox, 109, 112
acceptance
  agreement versus, 101–104, 110
  encouraging, 103–104
  key aspects of, 102, 110
  vulnerability and, 103
affirmations, 125
agendas
  hidden, 114–116, 134–135
  meeting, 70, 71, 73
aggression, in conflicts, 125
agreement, acceptance versus,
  101–104, 110
Allied Signal, 4
analytic skills
  in team decision making, 145–
  146, 148–151
  in TQM approach, 30–31
anger, mishandling of, 127–128
apologizing, 121, 135
AQP National Team Excellence
  competition, 5
assertiveness, in conflicts, 126–127
assessment of teams, 33–38,
  163–179
  and boundary management, 37,
  140, 168
  closing out a team after, 174–
  175, 176–177
  components of, 35–37

customers in, 170, 172–173
effectiveness and, 170–172, 178
frequency of, 168, 176, 177
goals in, 163, 166–167, 178, 179
key results in, 167, 178
management involvement in,
  168, 170, 176–177, 178
myths regarding, 164–165
performance measurement in,
  36–37, 169–170, 173–174,
  177–178
realignment following, 33–35,
  58
team charter and, 165–168, 170,
  174
360-degree evaluations in,
  173–174
tools for, 176
training, 37, 55, 56
atmosphere, assessing, 36
awards, *see* incentive plans

Barker, Joel, 154
behavioral skills, 43, 48–50
benchmarking, with other teams,
  74, 165
blasphemies, surfacing, 146–147
Blumberg, Melvin, on job sharing,
  75–76
boundary management, 37, 140,
  168

223